The
BIRMINGHAM CANAL
NAVIGATIONS

At the Heart of the British Canal System

Gas Street Basin, 1992
The canalside area around Gas Street Basin formed part of the first of the regeneration schemes that are still reshaping this part of Birmingham. In this view the towpath and side bridge have been carefully restored as part of the work.

The
BIRMINGHAM CANAL
NAVIGATIONS

At the Heart of the British Canal System

Ray Shill

TEMPUS

Inland Waterways Exhibition, 2002. The tug *Enterprise*, with three joey boats in tow, makes steady progress along the New Main Line at Ladywood and passes a traditional working boat and many other moored craft.

First published 2002
Copyright © Ray Shill, 2002

Tempus Publishing Limited
The Mill, Brimscombe Port,
Stroud, Gloucestershire, GL5 2QG
www.tempus-publishing.com

ISBN 0 7524 2767 9

TYPESETTING AND ORIGINATION BY
Tempus Publishing Limited
PRINTED IN GREAT BRITAIN BY
Midway Colour Print, Wiltshire

Contents

Introduction

There is a growing and unabated interest in canals. People find pleasure in discovering their past or living the present. New investment has influenced a canal regeneration fashioned in a myriad of forms. Disused waterways are opening up, existing navigations are being improved and new structures developed for the twenty-first century.

This study is dedicated to the Birmingham Canal Navigations, which is a canal system that lies at the heart of the British canal network. It is canal with some 230 years of heritage and unlike most navigable waterways, which were built to a specific route, the BCN was developed and expanded over a hundred year period. It is in fact a composite of four independent navigations and later-linking canals which served one of the most concentrated industrial areas in the country.

The legacies of these times are preserved in the existing waterways, tunnels, aqueducts and canalside buildings. It is a disappearing heritage, however, and many structures have been lost. Special attention has been given to this subject in the chapter that deals with the BCN network.

Trade was also an important influence on the canal. The coal and iron industry gave reason for its very existence. It shaped and fashioned the BCN, which made branches and altered its route to suit the coal and iron masters needs. The waterway was full of boats travelling its length carrying all forms of cargo. Coal was the principal cargo, often being carried in open Joey boats that were led along the towpath by a single horse. Once the mines closed and the furnaces were demolished, the branches were closed and left to nature.

A hundred miles of navigation have remained and, following the renewed interest in national waterways, have seen a revival in use. Private and hire boats now ply the waterway that was once home to the working boats. The BCN is a different world that now caters for people's leisure interests.

This book has been compiled to examine these subjects and to pay particular attention to the buildings, heritage and trade on the Birmingham Canal Navigations.

Help for this project has been derived from many people and the author would like to thank the following people and groups for their assistance:

Birmingham Canal Navigations Society, Bournville Village Trust, Mike Constable, Steve Crook, Jim Evans, Tom Foxon, Stanley Holland, Roy Jamieson, Lichfield & Hatherton Trust, Martin O Keeffe, Michael Mensing, Ron Moss, Phil Sharpe, Edward Paget Tomlinson, the late Patrick Thorn, Fiona Upton, Ned Williams, the staff of Birmingham Library Archives Department, Birmingham Library Local Studies Department, Birmingham Library Patents Library, Birmingham Museums and Art Gallery, Black Country Museum, Boat Museum (Ellesmere Port), British Waterways Archives (Gloucester), Cannock Library, Dudley Libraries, Dudley Archives Centre, Public Records Office (Kew), Sandwell Public Libraries, Stafford and Lichfield Joint Records Office, University of Salford, Walsall Libraries, Walsall Local History Centre, Warwick Record Office, Wolverhampton Libraries, Wolverhampton Local History Centre.

One
Maps of the Birmingham Canal Navigations

The original Birmingham Canal began as a waterway that linked the town of Birmingham with Wolverhampton and the Staffordshire & Worcestershire Canal at Alderseley. The main line followed the land contours and wound and turned through the districts of Bilston, Tipton and Oldbury, where coal and ironstone were mined. There were two branch canals. One was a short branch to Ocker Hill, the other wound its way from Spon Lane through West Bromwich to coal mines near Hill Top. An early map of the period that shows the canal is Yates Map of Staffordshire and *Map (1) Birmingham Canal Navigations 1775* is based on this survey. Boats travelling along the canal encountered two major lock flights. The first at Wolverhampton had twenty-one locks, whilst the second at Smethwick had twelve locks in total.

The Birmingham Canal might have remained in this state were it not for the coal and iron masters of Wednesbury who were keen to get better transport access to their mines. The Birmingham & Fazeley Canal Co. promoted a rival scheme that proposed a canal along the Tame Valley that joined the intended extension of the Coventry Canal at Fazeley and also provided a branch to the lower part of Birmingham then not served by a waterway. The essence of their scheme is shown in *Map (2) Birmingham & Fazeley Canal Company – intended route to Wednesbury*. The Birmingham Canal Navigations proposed an alternative scheme that joined their existing Wednesbury Canal and this proposal is shown in *Map (3) Birmingham Canal Navigations intended route to Wednesbury*. Parliament decided on a compromise and sanctioned a modified scheme for the Birmingham & Fazeley Canal Co., which received royal assent in 1783. The Birmingham Canal Navigations merged with the Birmingham & Fazeley Canal in 1784 and constructed the new combine set about arrangements for the canals to be built. The work included the making of a new canal through to Fazeley and Riders Green to the Wednesbury Coal Mines. The Smethwick Lock summit was also lowered and the remaining three locks at the Smethwick end were duplicated to assist the flow of traffic travelling towards Birmingham. *Map (4) Birmingham & Birmingham & Fazeley Canal 1791* shows the extent of the BCN once these works were finished in 1790.

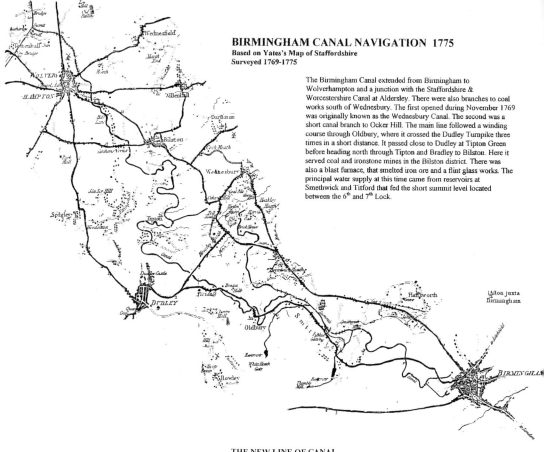

BIRMINGHAM CANAL NAVIGATION 1775
Based on Yates's Map of Staffordshire
Surveyed 1769-1775

The Birmingham Canal extended from Birmingham to Wolverhampton and a junction with the Staffordshire & Worcestershire Canal at Aldersley. There were also branches to coal works south of Wednesbury. The first opened during November 1769 was originally known as the Wednesbury Canal. The second was a short canal branch to Ocker Hill. The main line followed a winding course through Oldbury, where it crossed the Dudley Turnpike three times in a short distance. It passed close to Dudley at Tipton Green before heading north through Tipton and Bradley to Bilston. Here it served coal and ironstone mines in the Bilston district. There was also a blast furnace, that smelted iron ore and a flint glass works. The principal water supply at this time came from reservoirs at Smethwick and Titford that fed the short summit level located between the 6th and 7th Lock.

THE NEW LINE OF CANAL
AS PROPOSED BY
THE BIRMINGHAM & FAZELEY CANAL COMPANY

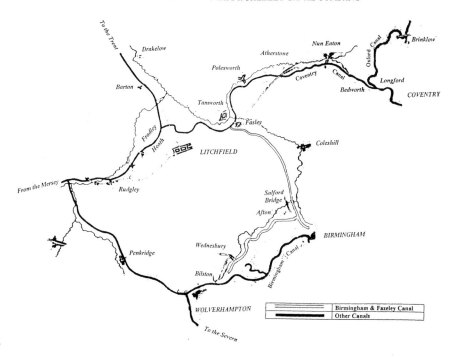

Opposite top: Map (1) Birmingham Canal Navigations 1775.

Opposite below: Map (2) Birmingham & Fazeley Canal Co. – intended route to Wednesbury.

Right: Map (3) Birmingham Canal Navigations – intended route to Wednesbury.

Below: Map (4) Birmingham & Birmingham & Fazeley Canal 1791.

**THE CANAL EXTENSION
AS PROPOSED BY
THE BIRMINGHAM CANAL NAVIGATION COMPANY**

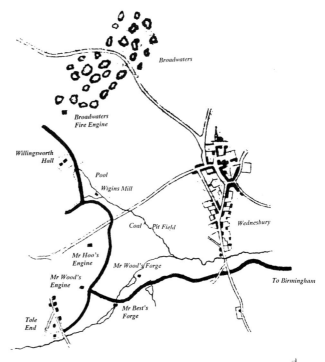

Birmingham & Birmingham & Fazeley Canal 1791

William Wrights Plan shows the improvements made to the Old Birmingham Canal following the removal of six locks at Smethwick that led to the lowering of the summit level. The plan also shows the canal extension to Broadwaters

Carey produced a book of *Inland Navigation*, which was published in 1796. He described every canal of the period and included maps of their existing or intended line of route. Every map also showed all the turnpike roads of the time, which can be identified by mileage numbers. The Birmingham Canal Navigations were featured on several maps and three sections of these maps are reproduced with this text.

Map (5) Birmingham & Black Country Canals (opposite page)
Carey's map shows the full extent of the Birmingham Canal as it was in 1796 plus the Walsall Canal and branches, which were then under construction. The Bloomfield to Deepfield Cut (below Tipton) is also included, but was never completed at this time. The full extent of the Dudley Canal is shown complete with the intended branch and locks to the Buffery. The original Dudley Canal was opened from the Delph to near Parkhead in 1779 and later extended through five locks at Parkhead and Dudley Tunnel to join the Birmingham Canal at Tipton in 1792. Carey's map refers to this piece as the Old Dudley Extension. The Dudley Canal Co. then obtained parliamentary approval for a new line of canal through Netherton and Halesowen to join the Worcester & Birmingham Canal at Selly Oak. Called the Dudley Extension on this map, it is better known today as the Dudley No.2 Canal. This canal was completed in 1798 more or less as shown on Carey's map, with the exception of the lock flight to Dudley, which was never made.

Map (6) The Wyrley and Essington Canal (page 12)
This section of the map illustrates the course of the Wyrley & Essington Canal, which was authorised by Parliament in 1792, and the Extension Canal of 1794. Parts of the waterway had opened during 1794 through to the collieries at Essington Wood and work was underway completing the remainder through to the junction with the Coventry Canal at Huddlesford in 1797. Parts of the canals shown on Carey's map were never completed and the line of the Extension Canal altered in places. The canal to Wyrley Bank remained unfinished beyond Essington Wood, whilst the branch to Lords Hay was diverted to finish at a wharf beside the turnpike road north of Bloxwich. The scheme to make a reservoir at Catshill, shown on the map, was abandoned in favour of one near Norton. Sneyd Reservoir, which also supplied water to the canal, is not illustrated.

Map (7) The Birmingham and Fazeley Canal (page 13)
The canal that linked the Coventry Canal at Fazeley with the original Birmingham Canal Navigation was authorised by Parliament in 1783. Formed as a competitor to the Birmingham Canal Navigation Co., the Birmingham & Fazeley Canal Co. had powers to make a canal from Birmingham to Fazeley, a short branch to Digbeth and an isolated section of waterway from Ryders Green to Broadwaters. The Birmingham & Fazeley Canal Co. merged with the Birmingham Canal Navigations the following year and all construction work was completed by the joint concern. From 1784 until 1794 they traded as the Birmingham & Birmingham & Fazeley Canal Co., then abbreviated their title to Birmingham Canal Navigations. Carey's map shows the route of the Birmingham & Fazeley Canal as built from Birmingham through Curdworth to Fazeley, but makes no mention of the short Curdworth Tunnel. The Birmingham Canal Navigations also owned and operated the section of the Coventry Canal between Fazeley and Whittington Brook.

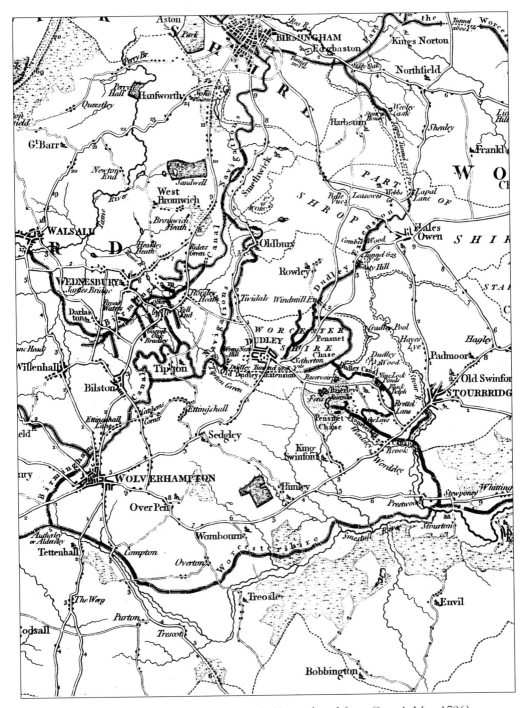

Map (5) Birmingham & Black Country Canals (Reproduced from Carey's Map 1796)

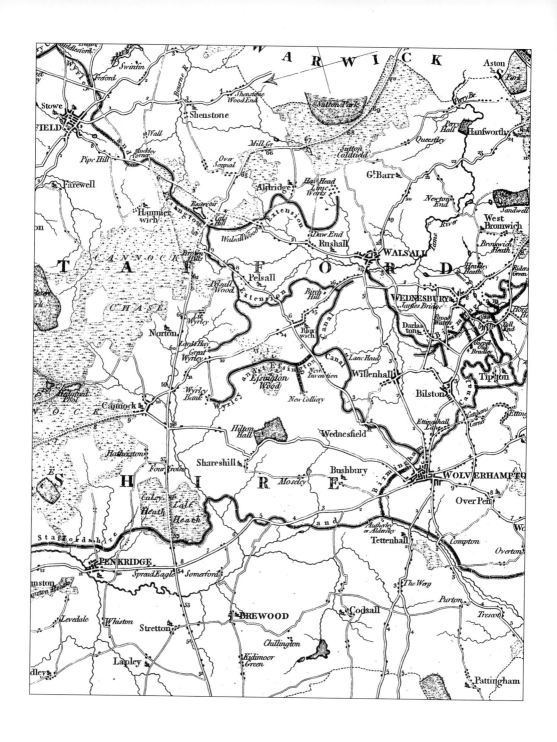

Above: Map (6) Wyrley & Essington Canal (Reproduced from Carey's Map 1796)

Opposite: Map (7) Birmingham and Fazeley Canal (Reproduced from Carey's Map 1796)

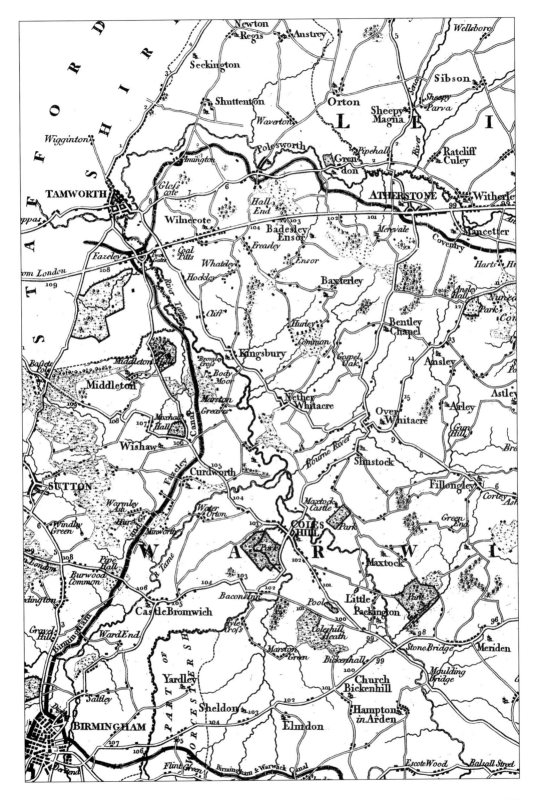

13

John Kempson produced a map of Birmingham in 1810. The plan shows the route of the Birmingham Canal as it passed through the town of Birmingham and wound its way through Birmingham Heath towards Smethwick. Kempson's map shows the canal arrangement before Thomas Telford's improvements.

Map (8) Central Birmingham (opposite top)

The southern terminus of the Old Birmingham Canal was located at the Old Wharf opposite Paradise Street, where they had their main office. The main canal then proceeded northwards curving around under Sheepcote Lane (later Sheepcote Street). Old Wharf was one of two Birmingham termini for the canal. The other in Newhall Street was at the end of the Newhall Branch near Albion Flour Mill. Parliament authorised the line of the Birmingham & Fazeley Canal to join the Newhall Branch at Farmer's Bridge. This bridge is shown on Kempson's map to carry the road from the Crescent to Sheepcote Lane. The Worcester & Birmingham Canal at this time extended from Birmingham as far as Tardebigge. They had wharves near the Old Wharf in Paradise Street, but the two navigations remained completely separate. The dividing line was a 7ft wide bar between the two waterways facing Broad Street Wharf. The Worcester & Birmingham Canal was by no means an isolated waterway at this time. There was a link with the Dudley Canal at Selly Oak, which afforded a connection through to the Stourbridge Canal, Staffordshire & Worcestershire Canal and the River Severn. At Kings Norton a second link was made with the Stratford upon Canal, which joined in turn the Warwick & Birmingham Canal near Lapworth and afforded other connections through to the Oxford and Grand Junction Canals.

Map (9) Birmingham Heath (opposite below)

The route of the Old Birmingham Canal followed what today is regarded as the two main loops that is the Icknield Port Loop and the Soho (or Winson Green) Loop. The waterway is seen to follow an extremely winding course as it followed the land contours. In between were valleys and hills that Telford spanned by embankments or excavated for cuttings changing forever the geography of the area. Kempson's map also shows the Birmingham Heath Branch completed about 1800 that terminated at Soho Wharf. This branch was built at the request of Boulton & Watt to serve the nearby Soho Manufactory. The canal also served two glassworks where flint glass was produced. James Taylor's Boatdock, although not specifically named, can be identified as the basin next to Spring Hill Bridge, opposite the Park Glasshouse.

The appointment of Thomas Telford as engineer to the Birmingham Canal Navigations led to a considerable improvement to the networks. The creation of a new main line shortened the distance between Birmingham & Wolverhampton and relegated parts of the Old Main to loop status. Both routes are compared in Map (10) BCN Old & New Main Lines.

Opposite top: Map (8) Central Birmingham

Opposite below: Map (9) Birmingham Heath

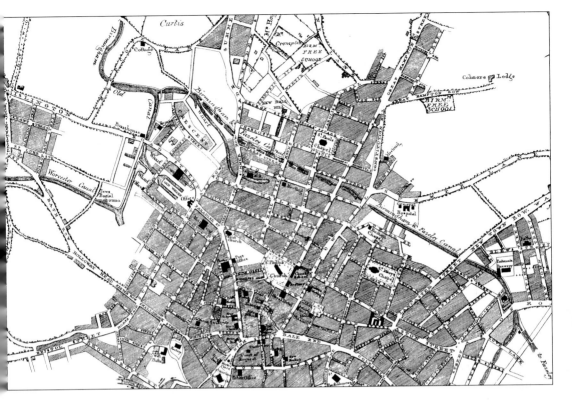

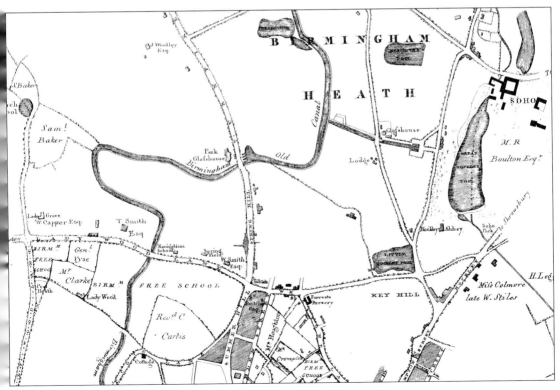

Birmingham Canal Navigations

Old & New Main Lines

Locks are indicated by numbers

——— Old Main Line
——— New Main Line

The Old and New Main Lines connected Birmingham with the Staffordshire & Worcestershire Canal at Aldersley. It passed through an extensive coal mining and iron-making district, which generated considerable traffic for the canal. The Old Main Line, completed in 1772, was over 22 miles long. The canal company made several shortenings to the route between 1825 and 1838 that became known as the New Main Line. These new works reduced the mileage between Birmingham and Wolverhampton and relegated parts of the Old Main Line to that of "loop" status, where the older waterway still retained a use serving factories and mines.

Map (10) BCN Old & New Main Lines

The Birmingham Canal Navigations were some hundred years in the making. The original Brindley Canal, the Birmingham & Fazeley Canal, the Walsall Canal, the Toll End Communication Canal, the Titford Canal and the New Main Line were all part of a sustained modification and expansion to suit the needs of industry. Then came the two important canal mergers that added the Wyrley & Essington (1840) and Dudley Canal (1846) to the BCN network. A series of further canal expansion followed that forged new links. Walsall Locks, the Bentley Canal, Tame Valley and Rushall Canal were all completed during the 1840s. Then came the improvements to the Dudley Canal and Netherton Tunnel Branch that were finished in 1858. The final parts of the network to be completed were the Wyrley Bank, Cannock Extension and Churchbridge Locks, which were constructed to serve the new collieries at Great Wyrley and on Cannock Chase. Hancox's map of 1864 shows the full extent of the BCN, the railways and the mineral districts of South Staffordshire and East Worcestershire.

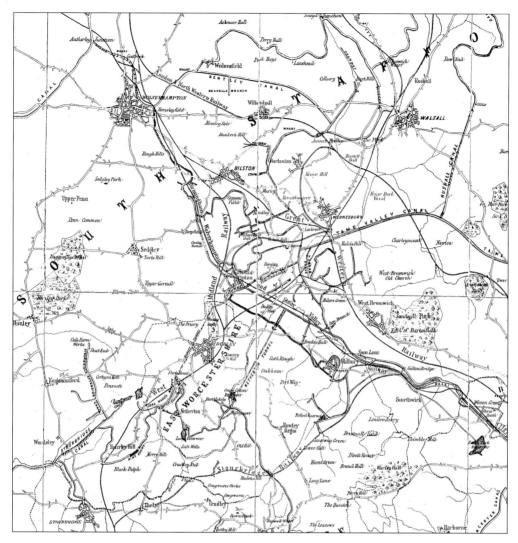

Map (11) Black Country Network
The decade between 1850 and 1860 had seen a time of intense iron production where between 120 and 130 blast furnaces were generally in production at any one time smelting iron. Gasworks were busy making gas and supplying by-products to the local chemical industry. Brickworks and fireclay works had benefited from the abolition of a tax on brick production and new works were being established to supply the commercial and housing needs. Coal was in demand everywhere. Every part of the local canal network was therefore busy with boats. This part of Hancox's map shows both the New and Old Main Lines and the many interconnecting branches that linked with them. Also shown are part of the Wyrley & Essington Canal that joined the BCN at Horseleyfields, the Bentley Canal and the Walsall Canal. Two canal company tramways are specifically marked. They were known as the Bunkers Hill and Hatherton Tramways. The Bunkers Hill Tramway, which served ironstone and coal mines near Willenhall, terminated beside a wharf on the short Willenhall Canal, whilst the Hatherton Tramway served mines near Birchills and terminated beside the Anson Branch Canal.

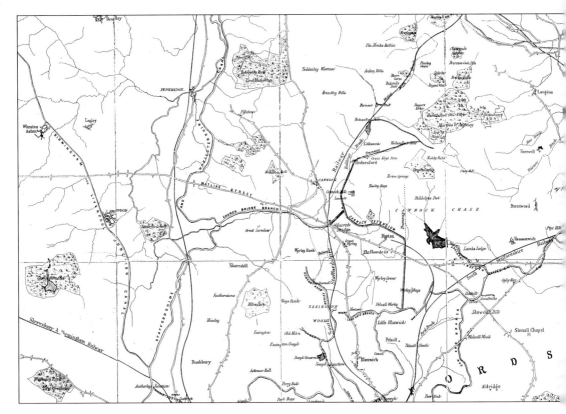

Map (12) Cannock Canals

The Wyrley & Essington Canal joined the BCN at Horseleyfields and extended northwards to Sneyd Junction where the Wyrley Canal diverged from the main route through to Birchills. This waterway climbed through five locks. The Essington Branch Canal rose through another five locks to a colliery wharf, but this line had been disused since before 1830. The Wyrley Bank Branch was a BCN canal opened in 1857 along a similar route as intended by the original Wyrley & Essington Act. The Cannock Extension Canal, which joined the Wyrley & Essington Canal at Pelsall, had been constructed in two stages with the final section opening in 1863. The thirteen-lock BCN Churchbridge Branch joined the Staffordshire & Worcestershire Canal Co. Hatherton Branch (or Churchbridge Branch) beyond Watling Street Bridge. There was a terminus basin at Hedsnesford where the BCN exchanged coal traffic with the standard gauge BCN-owned Littleworth Tramway. This in turn formed a junction with the LNWR-owned Cannock Chase Railway. The Littleworth Tramway had been originally made to serve Hednesford Colliery, but came to handle traffic for a number of mines. Both Cannock Chase Colliery Co. and Cannock & Rugeley Colliery Co. locomotives worked coal trains over BCN track to the basin. The tramway marked by a dotted line was known as the Norton Springs Tramway. Authorised by the same Act that enabled the Cannock Extension Canal to be built, work on building this tramway was delayed and eventually only partly laid as narrow gauge single track.

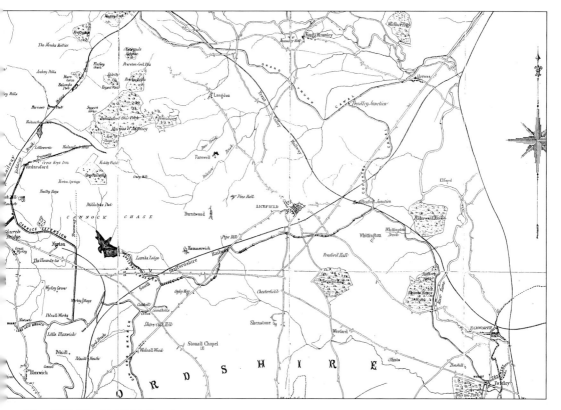

Map (13) The Lichfield Canal
The Wyrley & Essington Extension Canal was constructed through Pelsall, Brownhills, Ogley Hay and Lichfield to join the Coventry Canal at Huddlesford Junction. The level at Ogley was the same as that at Wolverhampton. Thirty locks were needed to lower the canal from Ogley down to the Coventry Canal. The locks were grouped in flights as can be seen on the map. This section of waterway was abandoned by British Waterways and the land sold off. There is now a determined scheme to restore this waterway to navigation again.

Map (14) The Fazeley Canal (next page)
The Birmingham & Fazeley Canal passes through the industrial and residential areas of Aston to Salford Bridge where junctions are made with the Tame Valley Canal and the Birmingham & Warwick Junction Canal. The route is then through Tyburn, where the Chester Road is crossed. Minworth then follows where the canal is lowered through three locks. Another eleven locks are then required to lower the level sufficiently to join the Coventry Canal at Fazeley. The route of the BCN then continued northwards as far as Whittington Brook where a junction was made with another part of the Coventry Canal.

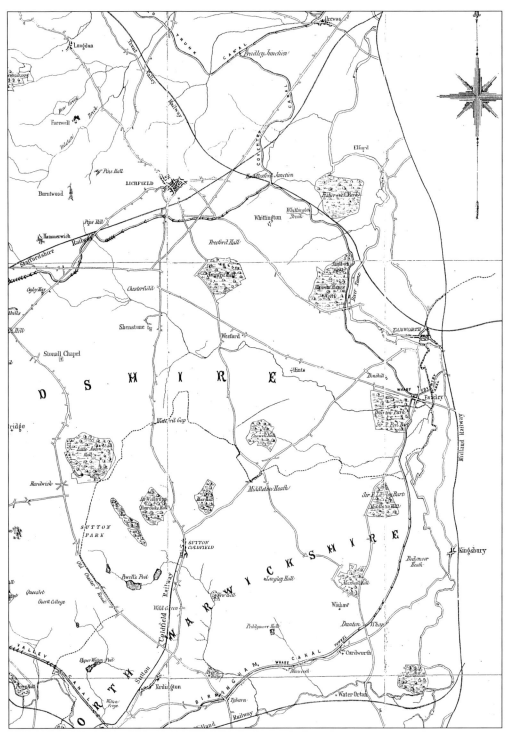

Map (14) The Fazeley Canal

20

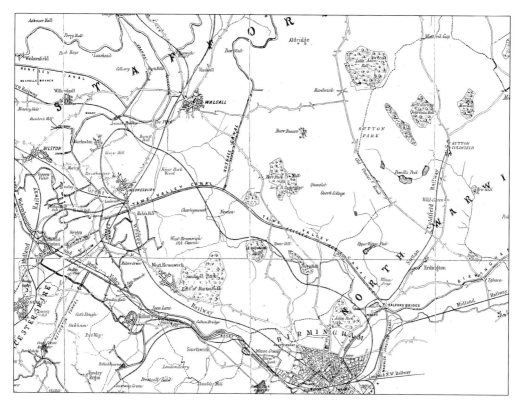

Map (15) Walsall and Tame Valley Connections

The Walsall Canal begins at Pudding Green Junction where it meets the New Main Line. It is a composite of three waterways constructed at different dates. The first section formed part of the original Wednesbury Canal opened in 1769 to Hill Top, West Bromwich. It diverged from the main route to Wolverhampton at Spon Lane and Spon Lane Locks also form part of the original 1769 route. The canal from Riders Green to Broadwaters was constructed by the BCN between 1784 and 1786 and was part of the canal to be built by the Birmingham & Fazeley Canal Co. Beyond Broadwaters the BCN Act of 1794 sanctioned the line of canal. This final extension was completed in 1799. The Birmingham & Fazeley Act and the Act of 1794 also sanctioned branches or cuts to various ironworks and collieries. Others were made privately, the Toll End Communication started as a private branch from the Walsall Canal to Horseley, but was gradually extended through to Tipton, opening throughout in 1809. A canal along the Tame Valley was planned on several occasions, with ideas taking different forms. The final route was formulated during the 1830s and finally opened throughout in 1844 to link the Walsall Canal with the Birmingham & Fazeley Canal. The completion of the Birmingham & Warwick Junction Canal at the same time enabled boats to work through and avoid the congestion at Farmer's Bridge Locks. Other links included the Bentley Canal that was opened in 1843 and joined the Wyrley & Essington Canal with the Ansons Branch, Walsall Locks completed in 1841 that joined the Birchills Branch of the Wyrley & Essington with the Walsall Canal and finally the Rushall Canal, completed in 1847, that joined the Tame Valley Canal with the Wyrley & Essington Canal (Daw End Branch) at Longwood.

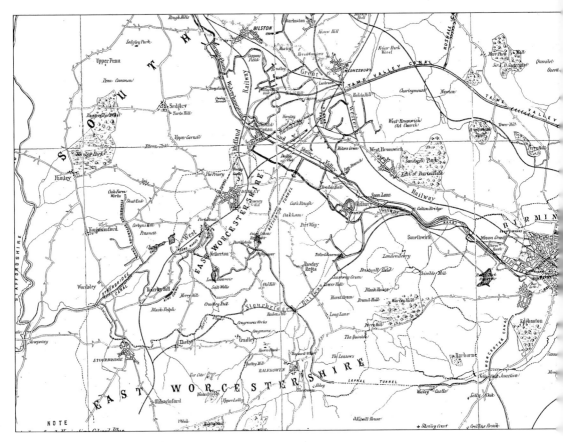

Map (16) Dudley Canals

The Dudley Canal was constructed in three stages and was owned by an independent company until 1846, when the Dudley Canal Co. merged with the BCN. The short original section formed a junction with the Stourbridge Canal at the Delph and rose through nine locks to a level section at Brierley Hill. This piece of waterway opened to traffic in 1779, which was the same year as the Stourbridge Canal was completed. The first Dudley Extension Canal was made from Parkhead through the Dudley Tunnel to join the private Lord Ward's Canal, which in turn formed a junction with the BCN at Tipton. This line opened in 1792. The third piece of waterway, the second Dudley Canal Extension, was completed from Parkhead to Selly Oak in 1798. Additions and alterations to the line of waterway were made in later times. Minor improvements were made during the 1830s where odd pieces of route were shortened and the Wythymoor Branch Canal was made in 1842. The most significant alterations were done between 1856 and 1858, when Netherton, the Two-Lock Line and the new locks at the Delph were completed.

Two
The BCN Network

Most canals have their roots in either the eighteenth or nineteenth century. Private finance usually funded the necessary parliamentary expenses, land purchase and construction costs incurred through the making of the waterway. Once the canal had opened for traffic then tolls for carriage of goods and rents for canalside premises provided revenue for maintenance, new works and dividends for the shareholders who invested their money in the venture.

The basic feature of any canal is the waterway itself. The channel used varied in width and depth. There was also a towpath which ran along one, or both, sides of the canal. Locks, where provided, also varied in width and depth and were the principal restriction for the size of boats used on the canal. Many West Midland waterways had narrow locks that allowed craft up to 7ft wide and 70ft long to work through this part of the network. Locks were the most common means of raising boats and lowering boats between levels. On some canals incline planes and boatlifts were used, but the BCN exclusively used locks. To ensure a constant level elsewhere tunnels, embankments and cuttings were made across the terrain. Aqueducts were provided for the canal to cross watercourses, railway, roads and tracks, whilst bridges also carried railways and roads over the canal. Water supply and management was another important factor. Storage reservoirs and feeders were essential to the working of the canal. Weirs were also required to enable water to be drawn off to avoid flooding. All these features are present on both working and disused canals.

Less common survivors are the buildings associated with the waterway. The infrastructure once included engine houses, lock houses, tollhouses, warehouses, workers cottages and company offices. All were once essential to the working of the canal, but with changing times many such structures have been demolished and all form part of the lost heritage of the canal. Many of the side bridges have also gone. The banks of the Birmingham Canal Navigations were lined in many parts by industry, which were served by a multitude of short branches and basins. Where these basins crossed the towpath a side bridge was needed to raise the path over the basin entrance. Once the works traffic ceased the bridge was usually removed or the towpath restored to the original level.

Towpaths were essential to any canal where horses, donkeys or mules were used to haul the boats along the waterway. On the BCN horse haulage was retained to the end of commercial carrying. The legacy of these times can be seen in the remaining canalside furniture such as the rubbing strips fixed on bridge corners, where boat ropes had cut deep grooves in the metal.

The Crescent Wharf, 1945

The carriage of merchandise was an important canal activity, particularly in the times before the railway network was established. The demand for merchandise carriage on canals developed towards the end of the eighteenth century when private carriers set up in business to convey goods along the waterway for a charge. Warehouses were established at strategic places where goods were delivered, collected or stored. The warehouse buildings at the Crescent in Birmingham faced the Newhall Branch Canal and were established by independent carriers during the 1790s and 1800s. At one time six separate firms operated from the Crescent Wharves, but with the decline in commercial carrying that followed in the wake of railway competition, several warehouse buildings were put to other uses. The Shropshire Union Railway & Canal Carrying Co. retained several Crescent warehouses for merchandise traffic, whilst Picton & Son also used one of the warehouses there. The SURCCC was in many respects the canal carrying department for the London & North Western Railway. They enlarged and altered some of the Crescent Warehouses. Fellows, Morton & Clayton who were their successors at the Crescent, may have done further work. Extra floors appear to have been added to the buildings seen in the above picture. The building over the basin once belonged to Norton & Co., Lime Merchants, whilst John Whitehouse & Sons and George Ryder Bird at one time owned the two warehouses respectively. When this picture was taken the whole area was intended for demolition as part of a civic improvement scheme. They were to last for at least another fifteen years before being pulled down. (*Bournville Village Trust/Connurbations*)

Portway Branch Canal, Titford
The Titford Canal was, at 511ft above sea level, the highest navigable waterway on the BCN. It was completed in 1837 to serve coal mines in the Titford Valley. This view is of the Portway Branch in 1945 when all the mines sat closed and only the Birchley Rolling Mills (right) might have required traffic from time to time. The abutments for Birchfield Bridge can also be identified although the intermediate span is missing! The Portway Branch served a number of mines which had basins at the top end. There was also a quarry that sent stone down to the canal. All trace of this section of canal has now been lost. (*Bournville Village Trust/Connurbations*)

Aldersley Junction, Wolverhampton, c.1945
Aldersley was the first BCN connection to another waterway. It was formed in 1772 when the link was established with the Staffordshire & Worcestershire Canal. In this view both BCN and Staffordshire & Worcestershire offices can be seen. The BCN cottage and office is on the right. Following the decline of commercial traffic, this building was demolished like so many other BCN structures.

Horseleyfields, Wolverhampton (opposite)
The Horseleyfields area of Wolverhampton had factories and works that lined both sides of the waterway. In this 1944 view the towpath is seen to rise over a number of side basins. The one nearest the camera was one of a pair of basins that served Mill Street Railway Interchange Basin, the next basin dealt with traffic for Bayley's Chemical Works, whilst beyond that was the Crane Foundry. The shadowy building on the right is the side of Union Flour Mill. British Waterways have since lowered the towpath to normal level. Bayley's Chemical Works were levelled and the site taken over by Crane Foundry, whilst Union Mill was demolished after a fire. A few industrial buildings with a heritage value remain in this area although their future is uncertain. They include amongst their number Albion Wharf, whose merchandise carriers warehouse date from 1828 and 1832 respectively.

Cannock Chase Reservoir, c.1900
This postcard view probably dates from about 1900 as it shows the part of the reservoir dam that was rebuilt during the mid-1880s. Cannock Chase Reservoir, sometimes called Cannock Heath, Cannock Wood or Norton Reservoir, and now known as Chasewater, was constructed between 1800 and 1801 and originally occupied some eighty-two acres of land. It was built to supply the needs of the Wyrley & Essington Canal, but was subsequently enlarged by them and later the BCN until the acreage was over 233 and the surface level, when full, was 499ft (*o.d.*) It is the only BCN reservoir to have two dams. The first built by Thomas Dadford had its height raised on several occasions to increase the capacity of the reservoir. Finally land was purchased to the north-west and another dam, sometimes called the Norton Dam, was constructed to fill a depression there. Cannock Chase received most of its supply from surface water that drained off the ground to the north. From 1855 a steam engine was installed to back pump water from the canal below. The engine house and stack is visible in the centre of the picture. Beside it is the smaller valve house that was use to drain water from the reservoir into the canal. The engine house was demolished in 1937, but the valve house remains. (*Walsall Local History Centre*)

Tipton Green Locks, as seen from top of second lock, 1957 (opposite top)
Tipton Green Locks were opened as part of the Tipton Green & Toll End Communication Canal in 1809, which formed a direct link between the Old Main Line and the Walsall Canal. Both sides of the waterway were lined with residential property. The canal was filled in and the houses pulled down. In this view the photographer has taken the shot from the top of the second lock looking towards the last in the flight before the canal was closed to traffic. It is still possible, however, to walk alongside the route of the canal and through the second lock chamber, which is still in place. (*Arthur Watts Collection, British Waterways Archives, Gloucester*)

Union Street Bridge, Tipton Green Locks, 1957 (opposite below)
A turnover bridge was built adjacent to where Union Street crossed over the Tipton Green & Toll End Communication Canal in Tipton. This bridge enabled the towpath to change sides and was constructed in such a manner that horses pulling the boats did not need to be un-pegged. The building on the right-hand-side was, at one time, the Union Flour Mill. (*Arthur Watts Collection, British Waterways Archives, Gloucester*)

St Chad's Cathedral and the Canal, 1897
Churches are an enduring canalside feature. This view of the Roman Catholic St Chad's Cathedral in Birmingham was published in the *Builder* on 27 November 1897. The perspective chosen by the artist was from the canal near the General Hospital, which then stood in Summer Lane. There was a large canal basin that served wharves there and it is from this location the view is taken. The passing boat is on the main Birmingham & Fazeley Canal whose towpath passed behind the wall. The road shown curving round in front of the Cathedral is Sherlock Street.

Gorsty Hill Tunnel and Tunnel Tug House, 1957
Much of the old tug house seen in this photograph has crumbled away, but parts of the wall still remain. In this view the tug house was still intact. It was used to house the BCN tug *George*, which took BCN day boats, or Joeys, through Gorsty Hill Tunnel to and from Coombswood Tube Works or Coombswood Colliery. Tugging was commenced during 1914 to ease congestion and speed up traffic passing through the narrow tunnel. Prior to the use of this tug each unpowered craft had to be legged through the 623-yard tunnel. (*Arthur Watts Collection, British Waterways Archives, Gloucester*)

Tipton Gauging Station, 1957 (above)

Canal craft were made to different dimensions and shapes. Several waterways undertakings adopted the method of calibrating boats so that a gauging stick could accurately verify their loaded weight. Adding weights and then recording the depth of the vessel above the waterline enabled the calibration of empty boats. Gauging tables were produced that listed weight against inches of freeboard. Metal boat indexes were then fitted to the boat's side, which the toll-keeper used to align the gauging stick against. The BCN, as a company, were slow to adopt boat gauging, but opened an indexing station at Smethwick about 1830, where carrier's boats were gauged. When profits declined more determined efforts were made to gauge craft. Records of these early indexing do not appear to have survived and it is not certain if gauging numbers were assigned. Following the completion of the second station at Tipton in 1873, all boats had to be gauged and a metal gauging plate with the gauging number affixed. The gauging number series recommenced at 1 and from this date both Smethwick and Tipton were concerned with boat gauging duties. (*Arthur Watts Collection, British Waterways Archives, Gloucester*)

Tipton Gauging Station 1993 (below)

Traffic on the BCN declined after 1920 and the Smethwick Gauging Station ceased to be used to gauge boats. The Tipton Gauging Station remained until British Waterways no longer had need for boat gauging. The buildings still survive by the top lock and are now leased to a metal treatment company.

Spon Lane Bridge, New Main Line (opposite top)
Canal bridges are a regular part of the canal scene, but these structures are subject to change. They were frequently altered through road widening schemes, where the old bridge was completely taken down and replaced by a new bridge, or additional bridges added to widen the span. At Spon Lane an additional bridge was constructed. In this view the footings are being made in preparation for the new structure. The industrial background has seen many changes since this picture was taken. Prominent in this view is the booking office for Spon Lane Railway Station (left) and the chimneys of Chances Glassworks (right). (*Sandwell Public Libraries*)

Oldbury Loop (opposite below)
There are many forgotten corners of the BCN that have been lost without trace. In this view the Old Main Line is seen from Halesowen Street Bridge looking towards Dudley. This part of the canal was reduced to 'loop' status as early as 1820 when the main canal was diverted under Whimsey Bridge to the Brades. (*Warwickshire Photographic Survey, Birmingham Public Libraries, Local Studies Department*)

James Bridge Aqueduct, Walsall Canal, 1983
Enduring features of the BCN network are the many unaltered aqueducts that survive along different parts of the system. This brick aqueduct carries the Walsall Canal over Bentley Hill Lane and the northern branch of the River Tame.

New Main Line, Dudley Port
A diesel multiple unit is seen crossing the railway bridge at Dudley Port one sunny afternoon in March 1960. The bridge, now gone, carried the Dudley Port to Dudley railway line over the New Main Line there. A bridge over the canal had existed on this site since 1853 when the South Staffordshire Railway Co. inaugurated the service between the two places. The main South Staffordshire Railway (Lichfield-Walsall-Dudley) passed under the canal aqueduct, which is shown in the foreground. This whole area had been built up above the natural ground level to meet the needs of transport. The canal was made between 1835 and 1836 and crossed the Sheepwash Valley on a high embankment, with aqueducts over Dudley Port and Park Lane. The parallel Stour Valley Railway was built between 1848 and 1852. (*Michael Mensing*)

Hednesford Boatmen's Hall and Mission Room (opposite top)
Many boat families spent their lives afloat, moving from town to town and wharf to wharf. This nomadic existence gave concern to certain religious groups who supported canal-side missions to look after boat peoples religious needs. Hednesford Mission was opened in June 1885 to cater for the boatmen who worked coal boats along the BCN to and from the Hednesford Basins. The building comprised a mission hall that seated 120 people, a coffee room and a reading room. Funds needed to construct Hednesford Mission were raised by the Birmingham centre of the Seamen & Boatmen's Friend Society, whose ministers held regular services there. Visits were made to the boats and people were encouraged to use the coffee rooms and reading rooms whilst waiting for their boats to be loaded. The photograph of the Mission dates from about 1900 and shows a party of children ready to be taken for a trip along the canal in a coal boat. The substitution of tugs for haulage on the Cannock Extension Canal during the 1920s led to a considerable reduction in time that boatmen spent at Hednesford and fewer and fewer people came to use the Mission. The building was eventually closed. (*Cannock Library*)

Birchill's Canal Museum, 1997 (opposite below)
Birchill's Canal Museum was built beside Birchill's top lock as a Boatmen's Rest for the Incorporated Seamen & Boatmen's Society. Between 160 and 200 boats passed through Birchill's Locks each day and the boatmen frequently had long waits. It was felt that the Mission building would provide a place of rest and recreation for the boatmen waiting their turn at the locks. G.R. Jebb, engineer to the BCN and Shropshire Union Canal, prepared the plans for the building which included a ground floor coffee room, kitchen and caretaker's room, whilst upstairs there was a large room intended for services and concerts. A subscription was begun in 1899 that had gathered over £91 towards the total cost (£350) of the building by the end of that year. The foundation stone was laid in September 1900 and the building was ready for services the next year.

Kingston Row Cottages, Birmingham
This view of Kingston Row has changed little in the last fifty or even a hundred years. At one time Kingston Row was a through road towards Sheepcote Lane across Farmer's Bridge. But Farmer's Bridge was taken down in the 1840s and replaced by Tindal Bridge a short distance away. The road system was altered and Kingston Row became a side street that provided access to the Crescent and Crescent Wharf. (*Birmingham Public Libraries, Local Studies Department*)

Canal Basins (opposite top)
The Birmingham Canal Navigations had a large number of basins and branches that served warehouses, wharves and works along its length. There were probably on average more basins per mile on the BCN than any other British Waterway. Each had a finite existence and only a small percentage of the total number of basins remains. Many basins served furnaces, ironworks or mines and, when these were shut down, the basin was frequently filled in. Some had extended lives as their purpose changed. The plan above was made to illustrate an alteration to the LNWR property in 1893. It shows a section of the BCN and Stour Valley Railway near Bilston. The two basins were made to serve independent colliery interests during the nineteenth century. This colliery land was eventually purchased for the growing Bilston Steelworks complex and Bilston Meadow Colliery Basin was adapted to load crushed basic slag into boats. Ten Score Bridge shown on the plan was made to carry a footpath over the canal.

Walsall Bottom Lock and Junction with Walsall Canal, 1983 (opposite below)
Walsall Locks were completed in 1841 and formed a much-needed junction between the Wyrley & Essington Canal and the BCN Walsall Canal. Local businessmen had long urged for the link to be completed and even set about preparing an independent scheme to build the link themselves, before the BCN finally stepped in and arranged for the construction of the short link.

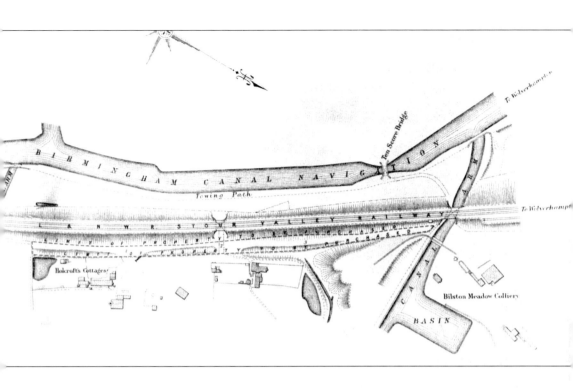

Walsall Bottom Lock, c.1960
A photograph of Walsall Bottom Lock captured in the early 1960s by local historian Jack Haddock. The view shows an empty boat about to descend onto the Walsall Canal. The building seen behind the lock was used by Walsall Corporation as a generating station before Birchills Power Station was commissioned. (*Walsall Local History Centre*)

Three

The BCN Cottage Numbering Scheme

Most canals still retain a number of cottages and toll houses, which are now a valued part of their heritage. The BCN has several such structures that were constructed for various purposes. Most common were the tollhouses situated beside the lock-side at strategic places and were home to the toll-keepers and their families. Sometimes the toll office was attached to the building and on other occasions it was a separate building. Other cottages lined the towpath, or were to be found beside reservoirs or engine houses. Accommodation was provided for a host of workers, including engineers, lengthsmen, labourers and clerks. Such was the complex history of the BCN that these cottages dated from different periods. Some had been constructed for the Dudley and Wyrley & Essington Canal Companies, others had been built as the BCN system was enlarged.

A metal number plate affixed to the side of the building identified each BCN cottage. Although many cottages have now been demolished, some can still be seen beside the waterway and at other places. The numbering sequence appears, at first sight, to be erratic. Two of the lowest are 27 and 28, which are houses on Edgbaston Reservoir. The highest, 271 and 272, are now private houses at Ogley Top Lock. Cottages on the Perry Barr and Rushall flight of locks all have numbers below a hundred. Those in Dudley, Tipton and Wolverhampton are to be found in the range 100 to 200, whilst Cannock, Minworth and Walsall are 200 or above.

How this numbering sequence came about is rather complicated and it seems that the basics of the scheme did not happen until the early 1900s. The BCN system continued to expand until 1863 when the Cannock Extension Canal was completed. From then until the turn of the century 159 miles of waterway remained in use. From an administration point of view the network was split into separate districts. By 1880 there were four districts. No.1 was the largest and covered Birmingham, Fazeley, Minworth, Perry Barr, Rushall, Ryders Green, Smethwick and Spon Lane. No.2 looked after Tipton through to Wolverhampton. No.3 was Dudley, Oldbury and Rowley Regis, while No.4 covered Walsall, Cannock Chase and Lichfield. Each district had an allocation of men and boats. Cottage rentals also came under their jurisdiction. Ocker Hill, with the engineering centre and main stores of the BCN, was also, at one time, classified as a district. They also looked after the cottages and houses attached to the various engines scattered about the system.

By 1910 there had been various administrative changes. Another district, No.5, had been created out of No.1 and No.4, which essentially comprised the eastern part of the BCN.

Ocker Hill lost its responsibility for its cottages to the other districts and Ocker Hill itself became part of the No.2 district. This was a period when canal transport, as a whole, was under serious investigation. Revenue was down countrywide and this was even reflected in the BCN accounts, despite carrying more than any other canal. A Royal Commission was appointed and every British canal was put under the microscope.

The process of self-examination must have had an effect on BCN management because improved and more comprehensive records regarding traffic were kept thereafter. From 1908, for example, the BCN maintained detailed records of all traders and the volume of monthly traffic each carried. A start was made on better and more accurate distance tables. The cottages owned by the BCN were also allocated numbers and records kept of the rentals. At first, the numbering was by district and not by the system as whole. Five separate number schemes were in existence by 1920. Eventually the schemes were combined into one. When this happened is not certain, but surviving records indicate that this was done after 1925. Those from No.1 district retained their original numbers. The rest, that is Districts 2-5, all had their cottages re-numbered.

A few cottages were built after the original scheme had been put into use. 58, the last to be numbered in the No.2 District was the wharfinger's house at Minerva Wharf, Wolverhampton. BCN records indicate that this house was constructed in July 1923 after the new wharf had opened. When the re-numbering scheme was commenced most were assigned numbers in a particular block;

District 1	1-99
District 2	100-149
District 3	150-199
District 4	200-249
District 5	250-299

The re-numbering was not always done according to the original sequences. There were quite a few variations particularly in the case of No.2 and No.4 districts. Cottage 1 in District 2 was 7 Castle Street, Tipton. This cottage became 100 under the new scheme. 8 was the cottage beside Park Lane Aqueduct that was burnt down in the 1990s. This became 124 in the Walsall District. The canal house next to the Birchill's top lock, which had been 11, became 206. The two houses at Pelsall Stop, which also still survive and had been 16 and 17, were re-numbered 211 and 212. The factors that decided these changes are not entirely clear, but it is reasonable to assume that the number sequence was adjusted accordingly to allow for demolished or sold properties. There may have also have been some consideration given to the geographical location of the cottages.

Wolverhampton Top Lock (opposite top)
The two canal cottages (109 and 110) beside the cobbles at Wolverhampton Top Lock must rank amongst the oldest surviving examples on the BCN. They have been altered several times. One had a toll office window incorporated within its structure that was removed and, as can be seen in this view, was in the process of being restored.

Rushall Top Locks (opposite middle)
The Rushall Canal was completed in 1847 and formed a link between the Tame Valley Canal and the Daw End branch of the Wyrley & Essington Canal. This view, which dates from the 1970s, shows the line of the Rushall Canal as seen from Longwood Bridge. The tollhouse (No.93), former stable block and boatmen's tea room, can be seen on the right. The Longwood Boat Club now use the canal here as their base. Formed in 1970, the club converted the stable block into a clubhouse during 1973.

Riders Green Bottom Lock and Horse Shelter, 1957
The Walsall Canal descends from the Birmingham Level through eight locks commencing at Ryders Green Junction. The bottom lock was near the Tame Aqueduct. The photographer has captured a scene now completely transformed. The bridge, that once carried the Great Western Railway branch from Swan Village to Dudley, the lock house and the horse shelter have all now disappeared. The only reminder of the horse shelter is a group of rings fixed to the wall where the horses were tied, whilst awaiting their turn for the locks. The Incorporated Seamen & Boatmen's Friend Society raised the money by public subscription for this and other horse shelters on the BCN. (*Arthur Watts Collection, British Waterways Archives, Gloucester*)

Churchbridge Top Lock, 1958 (opposite top)
The distinctive building beside the top lock at Churchbridge Flight is seen in its final years before opencast mining completely obliterated the canal and area around it. The locks were opened in 1863 and the tollhouse would date from this period. Churchbridge Locks were used to take coal from Cannock Chase onto the Staffordshire & Worcestershire Canal, Hatherton Branch, which it joined at Churchbridge, below the bottom lock. This tollhouse was under the jurisdiction of the Walsall, or No.4, District and was numbered 21 in the early cottage rental sequence. Churchbridge locks remained in use until about 1953 when they and the Hatherton Branch were closed to traffic. By the time this picture was taken, the Churchbridge Locks had already been abandoned and a concrete barrier has been made across the lock chamber to isolate the lock flight from the rest of the navigation. (*Arthur Watts Collection, British Waterways Archives, Gloucester*)

Churchbridge Top Lock and Wharf, 1958 (opposite below)
In this view Churchbridge Ticket Office and Canal Cottage are seen from the junction of the Churchbridge Branch with the Cannock Extension Canal, near Rumer Hill. The Cannock Extension Canal remained in water throughout until 1963, when the Hednesford end was closed to traffic. The main reason for closure was the constant cost of repair caused through mining subsidence. (*Arthur Watts Collection, British Waterways Archives, Gloucester*)

Bloomfield Junction and Bloomfield Stop, New Main Line, Tipton, 1957
The Old and New Main Lines diverged at this point. The New Main Line was completed in 1838 when Coseley Tunnel was finished. In this picture the New Main Line is the waterway that turns to the left and passes the Stop, toll office and canal cottages (52 and 53, No.2 District). The Old Main Line is seen to turn to the right and pass under the towpath bridge. The junction (and perhaps the buildings) dates from about 1850 when it was altered to allow for the building of the Stour Valley Railway seen in the background. Ox Leasowes Bridge can be seen on the right of the picture. It was built to carry a footpath across the canal. Footpath routes criss-crossed this area and were established means of communications for the local population in the days before public transport became available. Local people often refer to the canal stop as the Ox Leasowes Stop. The canal was made narrow here so that the passing boats could be gauged and their weights checked with the books kept in the toll office. The cottages and office were demolished after the decline of commercial carrying, but Ox Leasowes Bridge remained until the right of way beyond it lapsed. It was demolished by British Waterways during the 1990s and the Stop was also opened out to make the canal normal width at this point. (*Arthur Watts Collection, British Waterways Archives, Gloucester*)

Bentley Canal and Lock House, Wednesfield, 1958 (opposite)
There were ten locks on the Bentley Canal that joined the Wyrley & Essington Canal with the Ansons Branch, near Walsall. The line of the top six locks are seen from the junction towpath bridge at Wednesfield. The most notable feature is the canalside cottage, which was originally numbered with the Walsall District cottages as 36, but became 245 in the combined number sequence. Well Lane cottage beside lock 4, numbered 37 in the Walsall District, became 246. The lower end of the Bentley Canal closed to navigation in 1960, but the upper part that included the six locks remained technically 'open' to boats until the 1980s. (*Arthur Watts Collection, British Waterways Archives, Gloucester*)

Wednesfield Stop
This is probably a late nineteenth-century view of the Wyrley & Essington Canal as seen from New Cross Bridge. Two loaded coal boats pass the junction with the Bentley Canal, whilst another is seen through the bridge hole on the Bentley Canal. Toll offices might be incorporated within the structure of the tollhouse cottage or it might be a separate building as seen here. Tollhouse design varied; some were square-shaped like Bloomfield Junction and Catshill, others were octagonal in shape. The tollhouse that served Wednesfield Stop is partly hidden by the towpath bridge, but enough of its features can be discerned to see that it was made to the typical octagonal BCN design. Three of these toll offices, of similar design, were placed on islands along the New Main Line. (*Black Country Museum*)

Canal Cottages and Toll Office, Smethwick, 1957
The Old Main Line had a large toll office at Smethwick that was placed beside the path that linked the Old Main Line locks with the Gauging Station Island on the New Main Line. The offices were placed in such a location to overlook both waterways. All trace of these buildings has now gone. (*Arthur Watts Collection, British Waterways Archives, Gloucester*)

Four
Trade on the Waterway

The BCN was a link in a chain of navigable waterways that joined the North West and North East with the East Midlands, South West and South East of England. Traffic was both of a long distance and local nature. The merchandise carriers passed along the BCN, bringing and taking a variety of goods within the holds of their vessels. Most boat had specific cargoes, however, and coal was the most common type of goods carried on the BCN.

The demands of industry, as well as domestic requirements, generated a considerable traffic in coal, which only abated with the decline of canal-side factories and the closure of the coal mines. Traffic of iron goods provided useful revenue from tolls. The banks of the BCN, in the Black Country, were once lined with blast furnaces, chain works, foundries, rolling mills and a few steelworks, whose combined operations smelted iron ore to make metallic iron and then worked up that iron to finished iron and steel goods. The non-ferrous trade that included copper, nickel and zinc was particularly important in the Birmingham area, where alloys such as brass, nickel silver and phosphor bronze were produced by a number of rolled metal manufacturers.

Ironstone, mined both locally or imported from distant places, was frequently brought to the smelting furnace by canal boat. Limestone too was a common canal boat cargo. Local mines and quarries provided limestone for the iron industry and agriculture as well as the building and chemical trades. Other forms of stone such as the Rowley Ragstone, quarried on the hills between Rowley Regis and Dudley, was sent down to the canal to be conveyed by boat for road making.

Intermixed with the various ironworks and factories were the chemical works, gasworks, glassworks and power stations that used canals to transport fuel and materials. The chemical works and gasworks had a complex relationship. Gas for lighting and domestic purposes was once made from coal. In addition to gas, the process made a number of by-products such as gas water and tar, both of which were carried by canal boat for processing by the chemical works. Gas water contained ammonium salts that were extracted to make fertilizers, whilst tar distillation products included naphtha, creosote and a variety of dyes. Other chemical works manufactured and refined the acids so valuable to the metal industries, where they were used to clean surfaces as part of the pickling process. Phosphorus too had its part. The production of the safety match used phosphorus, which was extracted from its ores at Albright & Wilson's at Oldbury.

The use of electricity increased considerably during the twentieth century. All early power stations were coal-fired and used both waterways and railways to deliver the coal needed for generating purposes. Waterways also supplied the cooling water requirements for each generating station. From 1920 local industry became more dependent on electricity, which led to power station enlargement schemes or new power station construction. These needs in turn led to increased carriage from the collieries to the power stations by water, at a time when canal coal traffic was declining elsewhere.

Colliery Basin
Few collieries were visible from the canal towpath, but most had a canal basin where coal was loaded into boats. A group of coal boats are seen here in the drained basin of Hamstead Colliery beside the Tame Valley Canal. The reason for the drainage is not apparent, but maintenance work might have caused a section of the Tame Valley Canal to be de-watered. The colliery pit shafts were at lower level and coal was brought up to this basin by an endless rope tramway. Coal was sent by boat from here to various Birmingham works including the GEC at Witton. (*T.W. King Collection (courtesy of Mrs Ruth Collins), Dudley Archives Centre, Coseley*)

Foundry Buildings, Walsall Lock Branch (opposite top)
Foundry Buildings and a disused basin form part of this 1980s industrial scene on the Walsall Locks Branch.

Albion Mill, Walsall, 1983 (opposite below)
The flourmill was once a common feature alongside the banks of the BCN. Steam-driven mills were set up beside the canal to grind grain into flour and then bake the flour to make bread. Albion Mill, Walsall, was one of the last mills to be built and still remains intact today. Milling on the site has only recently ceased. Albion Mill stands beside the Walsall Locks Branch and had a wharf beside the second lock that enabled coal and grain to be delivered by boat.

49

The Old Wharf, Paradise Street, 1912

The Old Wharf at Paradise Street was extensively used for traffic from local collieries bringing coal to Birmingham. Boats lined the wharf-side to unload their cargo that was sorted and stacked before sale. Many coal merchants operated from this wharf, taking coal out by cart to both domestic and industrial premises. Old Wharf was established in 1773 and was closed after 1925, when the site was converted into a municipal car park. This view, which dates from 1912, shows the rear of the canal company offices. These offices were closed in 1912 and the staff transferred to nearby Daimler House. Demolition of the building had already started by the time this picture was taken. Once the offices had been taken down a new range of office buildings were constructed on the side facing Suffolk Street. Traders who used Old Wharf were frequently long-term residents, as businesses were handed down through the family. The boat seen in the foreground of this picture bears the name Anderton & Glover, a company who had been trading there since the early 1880s. They were formed as a partnership between Samuel Anderton and Edward Glover, but it was Edward who was to later manage the operation. They brought coal, which can be seen neatly stacked in the hold, from the Cannock Chase Collieries. The boat bears the number 16418 on the side of the cabin. This is the BCN gauging number and a study of the relevant gauging table reveals that the boat was gauged at Smethwick on 5 October 1898. She was listed as a wood cabin boat, 70ft long, No.7 in the Anderton & Glover fleet and had the name *Cecil*. When the Old Wharf finally closed, Edward Glover moved the business to Oozells Street Wharf. (*Birmingham Public Libraries, Local Studies Department*)

50

Old Wharf as seen from above Bridge Street
This view shows a portion of the Old Wharf and one of the basins crammed with boats. The wharf comprised two basins of similar dimensions made in the shape of a tuning fork. On the left of the picture were premises once occupied by Cadbury Brothers and the Eagle Foundry. In the centre of the view is a curved row of buildings that were known as Broad Street Corner, whilst behind them can be seen the distinctive Council House clock tower, known to locals as 'Big Brum'. (*Birmingham Public Libraries, Local Studies Department*)

Bilston Road Coal Wharf, Wolverhampton, 1944 (opposite top)
This 1944 photograph captures the view from Bilston Road Bridge. In the foreground is the Coal Wharf that belonged to W.T. Webberley, at this time. A collection of coal boats line the wharf, whilst in the background is Wolverhampton Power Station, then operated by the West Midlands Joint Electricity Authority. The canalside telpher can be seen as well as the concrete cooling tower that was part of the final modification to the site.

Thomas Clayton Tar Boat Dart *at Spon Lane, 1955* (opposite below)
This 1955 view shows the canal at Spon Lane. In the foreground is the Thomas Clayton Tar Boat *Dart*, which had come through the top lock of Spon Lane Locks and was now turning the tight corner towards Steward's Aqueduct. Various works are visible, as well as the public house at Spon Lane Bridge. Chance's Glassworks (right) and the clock tower for A. Kenrick's hollow ware factory are both readily identifiable. The M5 motorway construction was to completely transform this area. Concrete piers now support a high level motorway and the canal is diverted into a channel underneath it at this point. Little of the surrounding buildings are now visible, whilst the public house was demolished to make way for the motorway. *(Edward Paget Tomlinson Collection)*

Commercial Street Wharf, Wolverhampton (below)
Fanshaw and Pinson operated an extensive fleet of boats that brought coal from the Cannock Chase collieries to works alongside the canal. They had two wharves in Commercial Street that supplied both domestic and industrial needs. The one shown is of the yard nearest the Generating Station. The picture was taken before 1914 and shows a number of loaded coal boats waiting their turn for the wharf. Coal lies sorted in piles along the wharfside and a horse-drawn coal cart is positioned for receiving its next load.

Aerial view at Oldbury
The Midland Tar Distillery at Oldbury as seen from the air during the 1930s. Titford Locks can be seen in the bottom left of the picture, whilst the Old Main follows a winding route from left to right. Anchor Bridge, which carries the Birmingham Road over the canal, is visible top right centre. Also just discernible near Anchor Bridge is Hales Boat Dock. (*Martin O Keeffe Collection*)

Cox's Timber Yard, Great Bridge
Timber was once an important canal cargo. Both home-grown and imported timber would be carried by inland waterways to city timber yards. Cox had a yard on the Haines Branch at Great Bridge. This view shows a Severn & Canal Carrying Boat moored up beside their wharf loaded with a timber that would have come up from Gloucester. Notice the heavy-duty crane on the left, which was used to lift logs out of the hold. (*Sandwell Public Libraries*)

54

Rudder & Payne's, Albion Timber Yard, Birmingham & Fazeley Canal
Timber yards processed both English and foreign timber as well as being merchants for slate. W.D. Rudder founded the business in 1862 at Chester Street, Aston. Their establishment, known as the Albion Sawing, Planing & Moulding Mills, relied on both local canal and railways for transport of the various timbers. This view shows the wharf beside the Birmingham & Fazeley Canal for the English Timber Mill.

Rudder & Payne's, Round Timber Yard, Birmingham
W.D. Rudder & Son acquired a second timber yard in Chester Street to relieve pressure on the main mill. This yard had a ten-ton jib crane that was capable of lifting any size tree and placing it on a cutting machine table.
(*The above images were originally published in* Birmingham Illustrated, *W.T Pike, 1894. Collection with Birmingham Public Libraries, Local Studies Department.*)

Patent Shaft Steelworks, Wednesbury
This view shows the Walsall Canal framed by the Great Western Railway Bridge looking towards the Patent Shaft Steelworks. The wooden pitheads were erected over a pair of shafts working the remaining coal measures on Monway Colliery. Coal measure in this area comprised various seams including the thick coal. It was the thick coal that was taken first, but ribs and pillars were left to support the roof. With time the ribs and pillars were compressed enabling the miners to go back and work the coal again. These shafts were probably a second working of the remaining measures. (*Bournville Village Trust/Connurbations*)

Nile Street Foundry and Tube Works, Birmingham, c.1945
The Oozells Street Loop is now bordered by commercial and residential property, but there was a time when it was chiefly industrial. In this 1944 view from Sheepcote Street Bridge, the foundry and former Stewarts & Lloyds tube works are clearly shown. (*Bournville Village Trust/Connurbations*)

56

British Industrial Plastics, Langley Green 1983
The BIP plant is shown in this photograph to surround the Tat Bank Branch on both sides. The canal was established long before the plastics works was built, however. It was Thomas Telford who engineered the feeder from Titford to Edgbaston Reservoir and enabled the BCN to complete the work by 1830. The BCN later decided to widen the feeder through to this point to serve as railway interchange basin with the Stourbridge Railway near Rood End and later it served the works established during the First World War by British Cyanides, which from 1936 was renamed British Industrial Plastics.

Willingsworth Blast Furnaces, Wednesbury
The blast furnace was the means by which ironstone was smelted with coke to produce metallic iron. Blast furnaces were once common features alongside the Black Country Canals. They frequently received ironstones, iron ores, coal and the limestone flux by canal boat and also sent away pig iron by boat to be worked up into finished iron products. This view is of Willingsworth Blast Furnaces, near Wednesbury, with a pair of open boats moored alongside the pig wharf. The pig iron is seen to be stacked on the wharf, whilst the pig iron weigher's scales and hovel are also evident. (*Sandwell Public Libraries*)

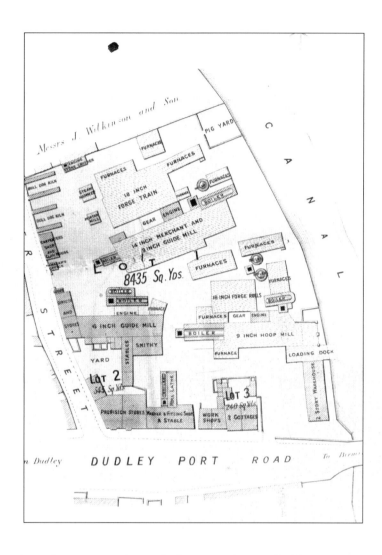

Dudley Port Ironworks

The many canalside ironworks took pig iron and reworked it to produce malleable iron. Iron made malleable by the puddling process was rolled in to sheets, bars and rails. It was a process that once heavily relied on coal at almost every step. Coal was needed as fuel for the boilers that provided the steam for the engines that drove the various rolling mills and the steam hammer. Coal was also needed for the puddling furnaces that converted pig iron to malleable iron as well as fuel to heat the annealing furnaces distributed around the site. Nineteenth-century ironworks were cluttered sites, often lacking symmetry, as additional mills and furnaces were added from time to time. The Dudley Port Ironworks is represented by the above plan and formed part of a sales schedule for the works. Dudley Port Ironworks was operated for many years by Plant & Fisher, but was later taken over by Skidmore & Co. The ironworks (lot 1) comprised an Old and New Side part that had various rolling mills and puddling furnaces in different parts of the site. The canalside loading dock and warehouse was located at the end nearest Dudley Port. The property then also included a Co-operative Store (lot 2) and a pair of cottages (lot 3). The canal shown on the right-hand-side is the Old Main Line, whilst the loading dock is built on an early canal wharf. This wharf had access to Dudley Port, an old Turnpike Road, and may well have once been the 'Dudley Port' that some believe was the origin of the name for the road and local area.

Plant & Fisher's Dudley Port Ironworks (opposite top)
This mid-nineteenth-century engraving depicts the Dudley Port Ironworks when owned by Plant
& Fisher. The view shows the works as seen from the Old Main Line. (*Black Country Museum*)

Netherton New Side and Old Side Ironworks, Dudley Canal (*opposite* below)
The district around Cradley and Netherton was noted for the chain making that was carried on
there. It was an industry that came to prominence during the nineteenth century and was aided
by the fact that the Dudley Canal was able to provide cheap transport for both the raw materials
needed for chain making as well as the finished products. The largest chain making concern
belonged to Noah Hingley, whose works are seen above. A collection of coal boats are tied
alongside part of Hingley's works that once had an extensive frontage on the Dudley Canal at
Netherton. In addition to these premises Hingley's owned collieries and iron smelting furnaces
that were all linked by the Dudley Canal. (*Dudley Archives Centre, Coseley*)

Manchester Works and Smethwick Locks (*below*)
Smethwick Locks formed part of the BCN Old Main Line. From 1790 there were a paired set
of three locks each that enabled boats to pass between the Wolverhampton Level (473ft od)
and the Birmingham Level (453ft o.d.). The canal in this view is seen at the top of the locks
and the entrance to both lock flights are visible. The one on the left comprised the original
flight of 1769, whilst those on the right, behind the boat, were the 1790 flight. Smethwick
Ironworks, sometimes known as the Manchester Works, can be seen on the left of the picture,
whilst on the right a corner of the BCN cottage and toll office group of buildings are visible.
(*Sandwell Public Libraries*)

Delph Locks, Brierley Hill
There were originally nine locks at the Delph that lowered the Dudley Canal to join with the Stourbridge Canal there. Seven of the nine locks were affected by mining subsidence and were replaced with a new set by the BCN in 1858. This photograph shows the 1858 flight looking up towards Brierley Hill. In the background the buildings and stack of a Brick and Tileworks can be seen as well as the BCN stable block. Brickworks were once common features alongside the local waterways, where surface clays were used to make red, brown or blue bricks, quarries and tiles. The boat on the canal appears to be carrying fireclay, which would have been mined at one of the fireclay works served by the Stourbridge Canal. (*Birmingham Public Libraries, Local Studies Department*)

Evered & Co., Surrey Works, Smethwick (opposite)
Evered & Co. had extensive works beside Smethwick Locks on the Old Main Line and another factory in Birmingham where a range of brass products were made. This advertisement, which was printed in Kelly's 1908 Trade Directory for Birmingham includes a balloon view of the Surrey Works at Smethwick.

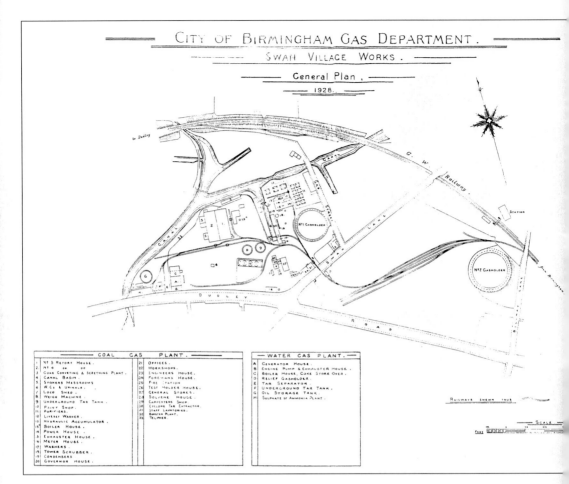

Swan Village Gasworks, 1928
A plan of the Gasworks, Railway Sidings and Canal, which shows the various departments associated with the manufacture of town gas.

Loading Coke at Swan Village Gasworks
An important by-product of the gasworks was coke. Gasworks burnt specific types of coal in retorts to make town gas. The process left a residue that was a mixture of large coke, small coke and breeze. Manufacturers principally engaged in the iron trade eagerly sought after these cokes. Some went to the blast furnaces were they were used to smelt iron, whilst the smaller cokes and breeze went on to the chain trade. This photograph shows workers loading a D. & F. Fellows boat beside the wharf. It is a scene that is believed to date from the time of the First World War, when women were employed in such work. Fellows were fuel contractors based at Cradley Heath who took coke from Swan Village and Windsor Street gasworks to Netherton for the various chain makers. Boat loads were delivered chiefly to Primrose Wharf, which lay in the heart of the chain making district. (*Birmingham Public Libraries, Local Studies Department*)

Bradley Loop
The Bradley Loop was part of the Old BCN main line that wound a convoluted course from Coseley through Bradley, Wednesbury Oak and Bloomfield to rejoin the main line at Tipton. Even this branch was subject to alteration and there was a short deviation made in the early nineteenth century at Bradley. This view shows the canal near Pothouse Bridge and canalside ironworks beside the original (1770) piece of waterway that diverged there. (*Bournville Village Trust/ Connurbations*)

Wolverhampton Power Station and GWR Railway Interchange Basin
This is the view as could be seen from a passing train on the Stour Valley Railway before entering Wolverhampton Station. The wooden cooling towers of Wolverhampton Power Station can be identified on the left the picture, whilst on the right are the railway sidings and the covered GWR Shrubbery Railway Interchange Basin. Shrubbery Basin was opened in 1855 by the Oxford, Worcester & Wolverhampton Railway and became part of the GWR system in 1863. It belonged to a group of interchange basins owned and operated by the GWR, LNWR or Midland Railway that transferred traffic between railway wagons and narrow boats serving works on the banks of the BCN and neighbouring waterways. (*Bournville Village Trust/ Connurbations*)

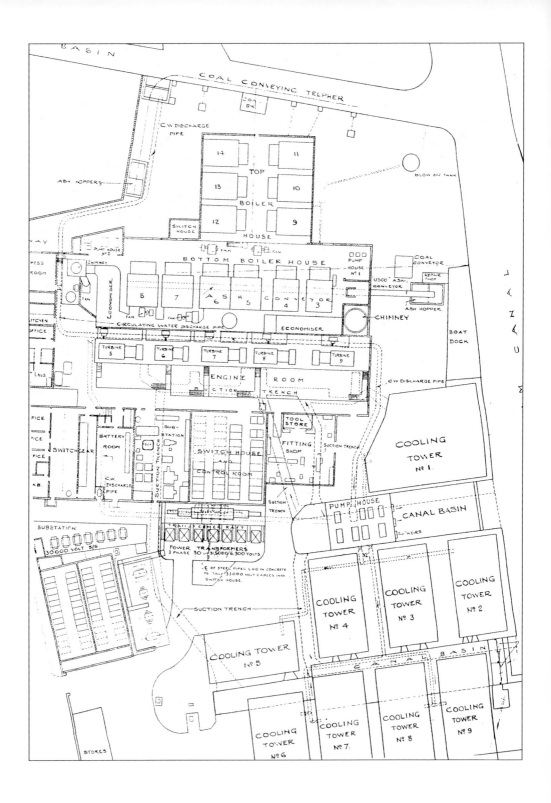

Philips & Son Bedstead Manufacturers, Speedwell Works, Sherborne Street
Birmingham's trade was frequently involved with either brass or iron and both these metals were essential components of the bedstead trade. Philip & Son had works in Sherborne Street that extended back to Morville Street where both brass and iron bedsteads were made. The above engraving depicts the square of buildings that comprised the works during the mid-1880s. The canal basin seen in the top right-hand corner was the terminus of the arm that extended under Sherborne Street from the Oozells Loop.

Wolverhampton Power Station, 1938 (opposite)
A plan of Wolverhampton Power Station that shows the extent to which this works had developed by 1938, when further extensions were intended. Power was generated on this site from 1895 initially to supply the needs of lighting and the Corporation Electric Tramways. The station was enlarged as demand increased.

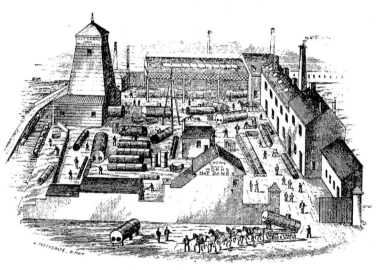

H. & T. Danks, Crown Boiler Works, Netherton
An 1886 advertisement reproduced from Kelly's trade directory that shows the works of H. & T. Danks, boilermakers. The Crown Boiler Works was an extensive establishment that lined the offside of the Dudley No.2 Canal near Bishton's Bridge. Their works adjoined the Netherton Ironworks that belonged to Noah Hingley and were opposite to the Shropshire Union Railway & Canal Carrying Co. boatage depot alongside Bishton's Bridge.

Five
Narrow Boat Variety

The common type of craft used on Midland waterways was the narrow boat. This craft was so named because it was adapted to pass through the narrow locks on these canals. The boats varied in length and width, but rarely exceeded the 70ft length or 7ft width permitted by the general lock dimensions. There was also a considerable variety in the types of boat seen on the waterway. The principal designations were that they lacked or possessed a cabin or if they were made of wood or iron. Those that had no cabin were called open boats, whilst with a cabin, were quite naturally known as cabin boats. Cabin boats could be of two types, those that had a large high cabin and those that had a small low cabin. The larger cabin provided enough space for living quarters. The smaller cabins provided little else but a shelter for the boatmen.

The cabin boat was commonly used for long-distance carrying of merchandise or bulk minerals. The hold was capable of storing between twenty-five to thirty tons of cargo. In the early days of the canal trade these craft included the stageboats and the flyboats. The stageboats called at all the wharves along a particular length of waterway and sometimes acted as feeders for the faster flyboats that called at selected destinations and travelled both day and night until its final destination was reached. Two crews manned each flyboat, one worked the boat while the other slept. Stage and Flyboats passed along the BCN waters, but the principal craft was the open boat. Many open boats were of a design local to the BCN known as the day boat, or Joey Boat. The Joey had a distinctive appearance as it could be steered from either end. Such boats were commonly employed in the coal trade, although they also found use carrying limestone and in later times mud, rubbish and salvage. They had a detachable mast and rudder and would be taken empty to the colliery wharf for loading, where they would be left until full with coal. The boat crew would return to fix the mast and rudder and then set off for a local destination. Such was the windswept nature of some colliery locations that small cabins came to be fitted to some of the Joey boats to give some measure of shelter for the boat crews, whilst the craft was at rest. Another type of open boat was the Station Boat. This type of craft, unlike the Joey, was steered only from the one end. Its role was to collect and deliver goods at the many railway interchange basins that served the BCN.

Canals are generally regarded as a means of carrying goods, but there was also a minor traffic in people by means of the Packet Boat. The principal Packet Boat route flourished between 1820 and 1850. It operated between Birmingham and Wolverhampton and only ceased when a direct railway was opened between these two places in 1852.

The railway network developed through Britain between 1830 and 1860. With the coming of the railways several subtle changes happened to the canal network and type of goods carried. Merchandise carriage was reduced to specific contract cargoes and the use of the flyboat declined. More people came to live on the boats and came to have them as a permanent, or semi-permanent home. These were the days of the Family Boat where the man, wife and children lived and worked within a restricted but tidy space.

There was a time when all boats were worked either by horses, mules or donkey. Men also did their share of bow hauling and poling to move the craft out of and into basins or alongside loading wharves. Experiments with powered craft using steam engines were applied to packet boats or tugs, which had a limited use from the 1840s. Steam engines fitted to a narrow boat were less common until the 1870s when a few commercial carriers started to use them. The internal combustion engine was an even later development. Yet following trials with boats fitted with these engines in 1906 and 1907, some carriers followed suit and by 1925 both tugs and motorised narrow boats were becoming common on the waterways.

The tug was particularly adapted to the coal trade on the BCN. By 1920 most of the early Black Country coal pits had closed leaving the Cannock Chase collieries as the principal supplier of coal to local industry, the power stations and domestic consumption. Coal contractors who supplied local industry and coal merchants who operated the wharves invested in tugs to haul trains of boats from the Cannock Chase collieries. Replacing in many cases the traditional horse-worked boats that were once common there.

Narrow boats fitted with an engine were frequently referred to as motor boats, or motors. Where they pulled an un-powered narrow boat, this was called the butty. The origin of the term butty goes back to the early days of the Grand Junction Canal that united London with the Midlands. This canal, which today is known as the Grand Union Canal, had wide locks that allowed pairs of narrow boats to pass through at a time. It was usual for two narrow boats to be paired together for the journey and when on the one boat, should conversation mention the other the means of distinction was that butty referred to the second vessel.

It is now common to refer to an un-powered narrow boat as the butty whether it is worked with a motor or not. Butty boats have a cabin and a large wooden rudder. When not worked with a motor they would be horse-worked in the same fashion as a BCN day boat.

The demands of the chemical industry led to a special type of boat being designed to carry bulk liquids and tar. Known as the Tar Boat these craft had flat decks and a cargo hold that held two tanks for the liquid. These craft were common sights on the BCN right up to the end of commercial carrying where they were used to bring tar and gas water from the gasworks to the chemical works centred around Oldbury and West Bromwich. The abandonment of gas making from coal led to a cessation of this form of traffic on the BCN.

Lovekin's Boatyard (opposite top)
The boatyard was once a common site seen alongside the banks of the BCN. Canal records show that traffic on the BCN steadily increased during the nineteenth century and by 1900 was at over eight million tons a year. All this traffic was moved by narrow boats made from wood or iron. Local boatyards built and maintained these craft. Many were made of wood, as these boats were cheaper to build. Boatyards were cluttered places where boats under construction and repair were distributed around the site. Many sites were simply plots of land beside the waterway that had few buildings. Moveable shedding was frequently provided to enable the builders to work under cover and some yards had the luxury of an overall roof. Much of the work was, however, done in the open air. Lovekin's Boatyard was located at the end of Rotton Park beside the Icknield Port Loop. The illustration shows their boatyard with wooden boats under construction. In the background are the chimneys and mills that belonged to Henry Wiggins, nickel refiners and rollers. (*Birmingham Public Libraries, Local Studies Department*)

George Hale Boat Dock, Birmingham Road, Oldbury
Several boat docks had an overall Belfast Roof to provide shelter for those who built and repaired boats. Anchor Bridge boatyard that belonged to George Hale had a covered Belfast Roof. Hale was a nineteenth-century boat builder, farmer and timber merchant, who also established limekilns and a coal yard opposite. As George Hale & Co., the boat, coal and lime business was continued well into the twentieth century. The boat dock is seen here, at the final chapter of its life, in an early 1990s photograph with the M5 motorway in the background. Shortly after this picture was taken the building was taken down and the timbers burnt.

John Jones Boat Society

Boat ownership was a costly expense and there were those who sought to even that expense through co-operative purchase. Boat Societies came into existence to ease the finance of boat purchase. The above is a copy of the front page for the articles of agreement for Jones Birmingham Boat Society that was formed in 1808 and met at the Waggon and Horses Inn, in Summer Row. Each member made regular payments to the society treasurer. Once £40 had been raised members drew for the right to have the first boat. That person then had to supervise the building of the boat, which was to be carried out at James Taylor's Boatyard. Each Taylor boat cost £86 and once the subscription had reached that amount the boat was handed over and the process began again with a second draw. Society boat owners continued to make additional payments thereafter and penalties were enforced for those who defaulted on payment.

Day boats, Walsall Canal (opposite)

The day boat, or Joey boat, was once very common on the BCN. Often made of wood these basic vessels were the work-horses of the coal and iron industry. They carried coal from the mines to the furnaces, foundries and factories with often only a rudimentary protection for the steerer. Cabins when provided were basic shelters, but adequate for the short journeys each vessel made. Early boats were fashioned out of oak with elm bottoms but BCN day boats were commonly made from cheaper materials such as pine. The most important feature of these craft was that they could be steered from either end. The task was simply of fixing the rudder to the stem post, setting the mast in place and securing the horse with a rope. The boat could then proceed on its way. A significant number of boats were metal and the BCN gauging registers refer to open iron almost as frequently as open wood. A large fleet of day boats plied the waters of the BCN. They required regular maintenance, which gave business to a number of local boatyards which were established beside the canal for their construction and maintenance. The photograph above shows a basin on the Walsall Canal, where two 'day boats' are moored. The boat on the left has a cabin and lies low in the water, as it is full with coal. The second craft, on the right, is a typical open boat that lacks any form of cabin. It is empty of cargo and rides high in the water. Scenes like this were common throughout the BCN system. Loaded and empty day boats were regularly seen at basins, wharves and moored along the canalside. (*Bournville Village Trust/Connurbations*)

Station Boat at Bromford

The coming of the railways gave rise to interchange of traffic between canals and railways. Interchange basins were established at strategic points on the BCN so that traffic from the many canalside works could be transferred to the railways. The BCN had interchange facilities with all the local railway companies. The craft varied and included both open and cabin boats. Yarwood's of Northwich supplied the LMS Railway with open iron boats between 1928 and 1938 often to replace older wooden vessels engaged in the trade. Many outlasted the station boat trade that ceased in 1954, becoming maintenance boats or being rebuilt with cabin accommodation for boaters. The former station boat, shown above, was photographed near Bromford on the New Main Line during 1980.

Coal boats at Pinfold's Bridge

Three loaded coal boats of the Joey type with cabins are seen here at Pinfold's Bridge, Wednesfield, about 1930. It is believed that they were placed here specifically for a series of photographs that show them on either side of the bridge. In this view the boats are shown heading along the waterway towards Wolverhampton. They are carrying small coals or slack, which is suited to the needs of the power station industry and may well have been destined for Wolverhampton Power Station. The boat nearest the bridge has the number 218 painted on the stern and this high number is consistent with the large fleet of boats that were used to supply Ocker Hill, Walsall, West Bromwich and Wolverhampton Power Stations. The West Midlands Joint Electricity Authority owned all these generating plants from 1927 until nationalisation of the power industry in 1948.

The boats in Pinfold's Bridge picture seem to be of the standard Joey length, but amongst their number may be a larger Wharf Boat. The Wharf or Hampton Boat was a larger version of the typical coal boat used on the BCN. They worked exclusively on the Wolverhampton Level (473ft) of the BCN where they carried coal from Cannock Chase to Black Country coal yards. Their dimensions varied but were always greater than the width and length of a BCN lock chamber, which restricted their range. Such boats tended to work to Walsall, Wolverhampton or Tipton and owners included John Toole (Bradley), C. Mitchard (Tipton), Ernie Thomas (Walsall) W.T. Webberley (Wolverhampton) and the Wulfruna Coal Co. (Wolverhampton). Individual boat lengths were anything from 76ft to a maximum of 88ft, whilst the boat width also varied from 7ft to 7ft 11in. The increased capacity meant that upwards of forty tons of coal could be put into the hold. (*Wolverhampton Public Libraries*)

Tar boat Soar, *Titford*

The tar boat was a common craft to the BCN, carrying tar and ammoniacal liquor from the gasworks to the chemical works that were concentrated alongside the banks of the BCN. The design was a distinctive one with a flat hold that contained two tanks to hold the liquid. The largest concentration of these works was at Oldbury where the Midland Tar Distillery (previously Lewis Demuth) was situated. The most well-known operator of tar boats was Thomas Clayton whose depot was also located at Stone Street Bridge, Oldbury, close to the junction with the Titford Branch. Clayton were not the only tar boat operator, other carriers included the chemical companies themselves, British Cyanides, Chance & Hunt and Midland Tar Distillers, all of which had tar boats. Claytons operated the largest fleet however. In addition to tar they carried fuel oil. This photograph, taken by M. Bunford, shows the *Soar* moored up beside the Shell Mex & BP depot at Langley on the Titford Canal after a six-day return trip from Barton. Claytons were slow to fit motors to their tar boats and all the early craft were horse-drawn buttys. The *Soar* was the first motorboat they had. She had started life as the *Lindola* for Fellows, Morton & Clayton in 1912, but was sold to Claytons in 1937 who converted her to a tar boat. (*Edward Paget Tomlinson Collection*)

The Watercraft Detachable Engine

There were many demands on industry during the First World War. Midland factories were in full production making items for the war effort and there was a heavy demand for coal. Canal and railway carriers were under considerable pressure to get the coal to the works as quickly as possible. The biggest delay for canal boats was loading. Empty boats were left at the colliery waiting for their load. A second delaying factor was that most canal craft were horse-drawn and therefore slow at getting their coals to the destination. As few boats were powered at this time Birmingham motor engineer, Arthur Hook, proposed an alternative solution. His suggestion was to fit an engine on top of the boat cabin, which drove a shaft linked by gears to a propeller. The propeller shaft also acted as a tiller and enabled the steerer to direct the boat in the same way as a normal helm. The arrangement was detachable and could be moved from boat to boat as required. It would be fitted to a loaded boat and speed its delivery by canal. Hook took out patents for this device in 1917 and also formed a company called the Watercraft Detachable Power Installation Ltd in 1917. His co-directors were Ernest Reid and Thomas Herbert Coggins. The engines were assembled at Hook's works that lay behind his house in 167 High Street, Erdington. Thomas Coggins was a coal factor and canal carrier who operated a fleet of boats that brought coal from the Cannock Chase Coalfield. The patent engine was fitted to boat 43 and made several trial trips along the BCN. The picture shows Thomas Coggins at the helm. Modern health and safety officials would no doubt condemn such an arrangement through the dangers of catching clothing in the revolving shaft. The company that developed the engine had mixed fortunes and went into receivership during 1921. The design continued to be used, however. The LMS Railway fitted one such engine to their station boat *Antwerp* during 1929. (*Birmingham Public Libraries, Local Studies Department*)

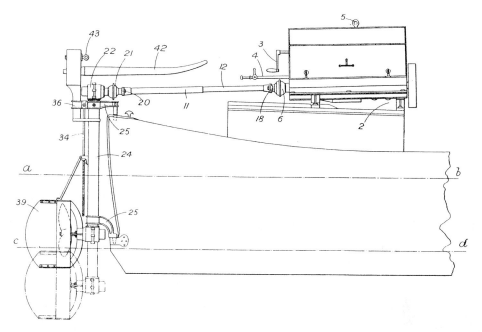

Patent Specification for the Detachable Engine
This drawing shows the arrangement of the engine. The height of the propeller was adjustable to enable it to be fitted to loaded and empty coal boats.

Legend

1 Internal combustion engine	11 Telescopic section	24 Shaft and casing
2 Bed plate	12 Telescopic section	25 Top and bottom brackets
3 Starting handle	18 Flange	34 Vertical shaft
4 Reverse gear	20 Flange	36 Member
5 Lifting ring	21 Ball and socket casing	39 Vane (rudder)
6 Ball and socket casing	22 Bevel transmission	42 Tiller
43 Lifting ring	A-B Laden water line	C-D Unladen water line

Steam-Powered Craft

The use of the steam engine to drive canal craft on the BCN was limited, but certain operators did use such craft from time to time. John Inshaw commenced a steam packet boat service between Birmingham and Wolverhampton in 1843. His boats ran, at first, on Sundays only. Fellows, Morton & Co., and their successors Fellows, Morton & Clayton came to operate the largest fleet of steam-powered narrow boats. Most of their fleet were powered by Haines engines, which were assembled at their Fazeley Street Works.

The Patent Disc Engine

Birmingham and the Black Country provided a home to many inventors and inventions where local engineering skills and a diverse manufacturing industry enabled many new ideas to be developed. The Patent Disc Engine was one such idea that came to fruition during the early 1840s. Henry Davies (of Birmingham) and William Taylor (of Smethwick) patented their version of the Disc Engine in 1836. Davies adapted the disc engine to drive specially designed canal tugs that were used on the Birmingham & Liverpool Junction Canal from 1843, hauling boats between Wolverhampton and Nantwich. The engines were built at the Berkeley Street Works of the Patent Disc Engine Co. in Birmingham and fitted to the boats at the Norbury Junction workshops of the canal company. Henry Davies moved to live in Norbury and following his departure from Birmingham the Berkeley Street works were advertised for sale. The advertisement was published in Aris's *Gazette* on 14 October 1844 and part of this advert is transcribed below. In addition to a number of disc engines a boat used for canal drainage is also mentioned.

TWO DISC Engines of thirty horsepower, THREE of twenty horsepower, TEN of twelve horsepower, TWO of ten horsepower, THREE of eight horsepower, SEVEN of five horsepower, and TWO of two horsepower, beside several Frames, two Water-heating Apparatus with Copper Tubes, several wrought iron BOILERS, for ten, five, two and twenty-five horsepower Engines; BLOWING CYLINDERS for Cupola; an excellent Five-Ton CRANE, by Bramah and Fox, and smaller Cranes; also a powerful HYDRAULIC PRESS by Omerod and Son, Blowing Apparatus, powerful bright Shafting, with pulleys, Brackets &c., a large quantity of Moulder's Boxes with other Foundry Tools; three Cupolas and Air Furnaces; Smith's Top and Bottom Tools, Tongs, 40-inch Bellows, Anvils and Vices, a quantity of Patterns, and other Effects; also an IRON BOAT, fitted with a five-feet Disc Pump, Engine and Boiler, for canal drainage; particulars of which will appear in the catalogue.

Early Canal Motor Boats

The magazine *Motor Traction* printed a full-page article in their 15 December issue of 1906. Entitled 'Motor Barge Development on Canals' the narrow boat *Progress* is described. The author of the piece observed that although motorised barges had seen considerable development on the Continent, the English canal barge proprietors had not seen their way to adopt the motor for transport purposes. The general 'bad' state of British Canals was attributed to the lack of enterprise. Now, however, one or two boats had been fitted with internal combustion engines.

The narrow boat *Progress* had been built by Norman Tailby (for Edward Tailby, timber merchants) of King Edward's Road, Birmingham, and was fitted with a 16hp two-cylinder paraffin engine made by Gardner of Manchester. The engine was run at 600rpm and a special type of magneto ignition had been fitted. *Progress* had already been tested on the local canals. It was sent into South Staffordshire and returned with a full load of bricks. It then went from Birmingham to Gloucester with a full load and returned with twenty-four tons of timber.

A further article appeared in *Motor Traction* on 24 August 1907, which again described *Progress* as belonging to Edward Tailby. In this piece the engine is said to be 15hp. On the previous Saturday the *Progress* had made a trip on the Birmingham & Worcester Canal. A number of guests had been invited on board for a trip from Breedon Cross to Tardebigge. During the trip, Norman Tailby, who had built the boat, mentioned some of the recent journeys undertaken. *Progress* had made trips to Sharpness, a distance of ninety-seven miles, taking six days to complete the return journey. Twenty-five tons of deal had been loaded for the outward trip, but the vessel had returned empty. Another journey was made from Birmingham to Ellesmere Port, a distance of eighty-five miles. This return trip was also accomplished in six days. The outward part took a mixed cargo, including bedsteads, and the return journey was with a load of timber. The boat travelled at an average speed of 5-6mph. Running costs including tolls, etc. averaged $\frac{3}{4}d$ per ton per mile. Normal paraffin costing 5*d* a gallon was used.

Other commercial carriers followed Tailby's example. Cadbury Brothers of Bourneville had their first motorboat constructed during 1911, whilst Fellows, Morton & Clayton decided to equip new narrow boats with motors from 1912. Prior to this date Fellows, Morton & Clayton operated a fleet of steam-powered craft.

BCN Tug, Norton Canes

Early tugs were powered by steam engines and were frequently used to haul trains of boats on river navigations. Steam tugs were also used successfully to take boats through tunnels, but their use elsewhere on canals was restricted. Chance and Hunt appear to be the first to use a tug powered by an internal combustion engine on the BCN. They had two tugs,*Hector* and *Stentor*, one of which was delivered in 1916. The use of diesel, or semi diesel, powered tugs on the BCN developed after 1919 when several coal contractors had tugs made. In essence a tug was simply a pulling machine and had no space for cargo like a traditional narrow boat, but it was powerful enough to pull a train of boats and this fact alone was enough to retain canal traffic to the collieries on Cannock Chase. Every open boat had hitherto required a boat horse to work it with a crew of two. Boats worked by a tug needed only a steerer to guide their progress along the canal. The waiting time for loading at the collieries was also eliminated as empty boats could be left by the tug, whilst loaded craft were collected. In this postcard view a tug is seen bringing a train of three loaded boats along the Cannock Extension Canal at Norton Canes. (*Edward Paget Tomlinson Collection*)

Elements Boat near Coleshill

The working boat on narrow canals incorporated the same basic features. There was a long cargo hold and a cabin at the rear. An additional front cabin was optional. Whether worked by a horse or fitted with a motor, such boats were regular sights on local waterways until the 1960s. They carried all forms of goods that ranged from minerals to merchandise. In this view captured by J.G. Parkinson in July 1955 a Thomas & Samuel element boat is seen travelling empty along the Birmingham & Fazeley Canal near Curdworth en route to Fazeley. It was returning empty from the GEC at Witton to collect another load of coal from the mines beside either the Coventry or Ashby Canal. (*Edward Paget Tomlinson Collection*)

Caggy Stevens' Tug, Gas Street, 1993 (above)
Allan Stevens' tug *Caggy* is seen moored at Gas Street in 1993.

The tar boat Dane (left)
Dane is now in private ownership. A significant number of working boats remain in private ownership, where they have been carefully restored to pristine condition. Most are looked after better now than while working on the waterways.

Caggy Stevens' boat with Don Payne and horse 'Candy'
Canal carrying in later years was often reduced to movement of spoil and rubbish. Caggy Stevens continued this trade long after other commercial carriers had transferred to road haulage or given up carrying altogether. He used a varied collection of boats that were usually pulled about by his tug, but he did arrange the odd horse boat movement from time to time. This photograph was taken in the mid-1970s and shows Don Payne with 'Candy' drawing a boat along the Birmingham Canal New Main Line near Spon Lane Bridge. (*Geoff Bennet*)

Butty Raymond *at Black Country Museum*

Wooden boats need regular maintenance. Ice, rain and the everyday knock and bumps sustained during an average working day take an inevitable toll on the structure. This 1990s photograph of the butty boat *Raymond* is evidence enough of the state that a wooden boat can deteriorate to. Built at Braunston in 1958, for the coal contractor Samuel Barlow, of Glascote, the *Raymond* was the youngest of their fleet. *Raymond* spent much of her working life taking coal along the Grand Union Canal for both Barlows and Blue Line. In the later years of private ownership, this boat was moored at the Black Country Museum where this picture was taken. Extensive repairs were carried out to her during the late 1990s, when a considerable portion of the structure was replaced. It is perhaps now more new than old, but such was the way, with wooden craft parts being replaced throughout their working life and, at the end of it, little original might remain.

NOTICE.

THE EUPHRATES PACKET COMPANY will commence running their packet on Monday, October 23, 1837, from Deepfield to Birmingham, in two hours and a half.

On Mondays, Tuesdays, Thursdays, Fridays, and Saturdays, for the accommodation of passengers and conveyance of parcels, leaves Mr. RICHARD THOMPSON'S, BOAT INN, Deepfield, at eight o'clock in the morning, through Tipton Green, Dudley Port, Tividale, Oldbury, Spon Lane, and Smethwick, to Mr. JOHN O. WILLIAMS'S, WAGGON AND HORSES, Friday Bridge, Birmingham, and returns at five o'clock the same evening. Also on Wednesdays, leaves Mr. JAMES ASTON'S, FOUNTAIN INN, Tipton Green, at half-past eight o'clock in the morning, through Coseley, Deepfield, and Millfield, in one hour, to Wolverhampton, and returns at four o'clock the same evening.

Passenger-carrying packet boats operated from Birmingham along the canal to Tipton and later Wolverhampton. This advert announced the new service offered by Thomas Monk from Deepfields in October 1837. (*Wolverhampton Chronicle, October 1837*)

Matty's Yard, Coseley

The district, known as Deepfields, is part of Coseley. The BCN New Main Line passes through Deepfields on the section that lies between Coseley Tunnel and the Deepfields Junction where both the Old and New Lines join and follow the same course through Bilston to Wolverhampton. This section of waterway was opened as part of the New Main Line through the completion of Coseley Tunnel in 1838, but prior to that had been a short branch off the Old Main Line. Authority to build a tunnel through the hillside at Coseley had been granted in 1794, as the Bloomfield to Deepfield Cut sections of waterway had been constructed at both ends before 1800. A start was even made on the tunnel, with construction shafts being sunk at the Deepfields end, but the work remained unfinished and it was not until the mid-1820s that Thomas Telford planned the New Main Line route. The canal here has all the attributes of a Telford waterway, being straight and wide. The normal double towpath has been dispensed with, however, to allow for the needs of industry. This section of the canal once served the Cannon Iron Foundry, Priorsfield Foundry and Priorsfield Furnaces. In this 1998 view, the line of the canal is shown looking towards Hills Bridge, Deepfields. The arm on the right once extended under Biddings Lane to serve Priorsfield Furnaces and also had wharf space for Priorsfield Brickworks, Wright's Coal Wharf and Etheridge's Lime Works. At one time this arm belonged to a group of basins that radiated from the main canal at this point. Most some served as wharves for tram roads bringing coal from pits shafts on nearby Ettingshall Colliery. During the 1950s the arm was home to Walton's boat building yard and was also a base for Alfred Matty & Sons canal contractor. Matty's were associated with various canal maintenance schemes until the early 1990s when their yard closed and now is principally a crane hire base. James Walton established the boatyard here about 1951. He had started in the trade aged fourteen as an apprentice boat builder at John Toole's yard at Bilston and worked his way up to foreman of that yard. His trade was thus one of maintaining and building Joey boats in the 1930s and 1940s. James Walton and son Geoffrey continued these skills at Coseley and from 1958 specialised in the building of canal cruisers and other pleasure craft.

Valencia Wharf, Oldbury

A part of Valencia Wharf, Oldbury, seen here in 1996, was leased by Les Allen & Sons, who made and repaired steel canal boats for the leisure trade. Les Allen had learned his trade working for Spencer Abbott, coal contractors, at Salford Bridge, Birmingham, but had set up at Oldbury in 1951 to continue the business of boat repair and construction. Les Allen, like James Walton, chose to diversify into the pleasure boat trade. Sons Bob and John carried on the business until 1997. Modern Valencia Wharf was restricted to two short basins near Whimsey Bridge on the Old Main Line. Originally there were five basins, the first of which was a long basin that extended as far as Valentia Colliery. This long basin was sometimes called the Valentia Arm and sometimes the Churchbridge Arm. At the end nearest the Old Main Line were located Valentia Wharf and a boat dock used to repair and maintain Chance & Hunt's fleet of acid, gas water and tar-carrying craft. Valentia Arm was completely filled in, but basin No.2 (Radnall Field Brickworks) and basin No.3 (W.E. Chance's Oldbury Glassworks) remained. They were leased to T. & S. Element's canal contractors and subsequently taken over by Les Allen. The name Valentia changed to Valencia possibly about this time.

The following newspaper extract refers to an interview with Les Allen, boat builder at Salford Bridge in 1949. Spencer Abbott, who once operated a large fleet of boats bringing coal to Birmingham, employed Les to maintain their fleet. It is an account that effectively summarises the lot of the carrying trade at the time.

Despite the decline in canal traffic, a Birmingham firm of boat builders at Salford Bridge is still making new barges. Five barges have been recently built and delivered to the British Electricity Authority and the sixth is nearing completion.

Veteran craftsman Leslie Allen who followed his father into the boat-building business and whose son joined the business this year, showed me some of the features of the barges. 'The design hasn't altered in the last 50 years,' he said. 'We still make them of English elm and English oak, the elm for the bottom, and the oak for the sides. They're carvel built with caulked seams.' 'Their size hasn't changed either, they're still the regular 71ft long with a 7ft 1in beam, and they draw 10in empty and about 2ft 6in loaded.'

'I think perhaps the only difference is in the oakum we used for the caulking. It used to be picked by prisoners but now they don't do it any more for punishment so we have to use machine picked oakum and it is not so good...'

The Costs

If the design of the barges has not changed, their cost has. One of these standard boats cost about £120 before the first war. By 1921 the cost had risen to around £250 and the barges, which are being built today cost between £600 and £650 each.

The barge builders are apprehensive about the future of the canals. 'I suppose that there is only about a tenth of the tonnage carried on the canals today as there was in 1921 – a peak year', the boat builder said. 'Take my company for instance. Then we had over 150 barges on the water, all in use, but today we are down to three. It is not worth while spending money to repair the old barges; the waterways just can't compete with the road transport people.'

'I always thought that barge transport was the cheapest,' I said.

'It was once, but there are so many labour charges today,' Les Allen declared. 'Most of the cargo is coal, and it has to be carried to the boats. Then we have to pay a surcharge of 1s 6d a ton to the National Coal Board, when the coal's loaded. Modern factories are not built with their boiler rooms next to the canal like they used to, so coal often has to be unloaded and carried some distance to the coal dump.

'Then there is the question of time. To make one delivery it takes a barge two days: a day to go and pick the coal up and a day to take it to its destination and unload it. It is true that the barge will carry twenty-six tons but four lorries could do the job in a morning.'

Losing Battle

When I said that I thought that the standard barges should carry thirty tons, the expert smiled sadly.

'They should but we daren't put more than twenty-six tons in them today because the canals need dredging and the extra four tons would ground them. That's a loss of four tons a journey for each barge.'

It was refreshing to hear praise of a Government department when Les Allen told me, 'British Waterways are doing everything to encourage canal traffic although I'm afraid that they are fighting a losing battle. I reckon myself that canals are Victorian, completely out of date today. Of course, there are things to be said for them, canals are just the thing for long distance work with heavy loads, but they're useless when there's any need for speed.'

Rowing Boats, Leasowes Park
Leisure craft use on the BCN during the days of the working boat was restricted to odd corners of the navigation. The Dudley Canal beyond Mucklows Hill was one such place that saw little navigation once Lapal Tunnel had closed. The waterway that passed through the Leasowes Park to the tunnel was used by rowing boats, seen here tied up beside the landing stage at Mucklows Hill. (*Steve Crook Collection*)

Tugs beside NIA (opposite top)
The 'pusher' tug was the latest form of canal craft to be used on the BCN. Their role is essentially maintenance, where mud hoppers were propelled about the network. Hardy Spicer, however, had a job in the 1960s that used this type of tug to take components from a factory in Deakins Avenue, Witton, along the Tame Valley Canal and Birmingham & Fazeley Canal to their new factory at Erdington. In this 1992 photograph a pair of pusher tugs involved in environmental dredging pass the NIA en route to their next job.

Mud hoppers, Bellis & Morcam Works (opposite below)
Mud hoppers moored at Icknield Square Junction in 1992 where the Icknield Port Loop diverges from the New Main Line. These boats were employed on environmental dredging work around Gas Street and the New Main Line. Canal mud in this area had been contaminated with a variety of toxic substances through some 200 years of trade on the waterways. The mud was dredged out and taken to the disused Bellis & Morcam factory (seen behind the boats) as part of a general clean up program. Here the waste was stored and sorted before safe disposal.

BCN maintenance craft near Galton House
Not all canal locations were spoilt by industry. This wooded view is taken along the Old Main
Line facing the grounds of Galton House. A working boat is seen approaching from distant
Smethwick while a BCN maintenance joey and spoon dredger come alongside the offside bank
of the canal. (*Smethwick Public Libraries*)

BCN Maintenance Craft

The Birmingham Canal Navigations operated a fleet of up to 150 maintenance craft that were allocated to various districts. They varied in length and width according to purpose. Many were 'open iron', 'open wood', 'cabin iron' or 'cabin wood' craft, but there were other types. The following is a list of special craft extracted from a 1923 list of BCN maintenance vessels.

BCN No.	BCN Gauge	Type	Year
14	22276	Cabin Iron Frigate	1890
25	20544	Cabin Iron Deck	1908
27	22350	Cabin Iron Dredger	1888
33	22998	Cabin Iron Dredger	1902
49	18891	Cabin Iron Dredger	c.1877
51	16191	Cabin Iron Dredger	1886
52	18571	Cabin Iron Deck	1886
56	18416	Cabin Iron Dredger	1886
61	19061	Cabin Iron Tunnel Dredger	1886
84	23271	Cabin Wood Dredger	1899
97	16342	Cabin Iron Dredger	1898
118	22321	Cabin Iron Dredger	1885
119	14454	Cabin Iron Dredger	1885
120	20790	Cabin Iron Dredger	1885

Other craft were built specially as ice boats. From 1923 a new type of maintenance boat, the mud hopper, came to be used. These craft can be still seen in use today by British Waterways.

Spoon Dredger, Dudley Canal
The spoon dredger was a useful tool for the BCN maintenance fleet before the invention of mechanical diggers. Small but sturdy, these craft were used to dig out the mud that came to clog basins and wharves. Planks were fitted along both sides of the vessel to enable the labourers to stand there whilst dredging the bottom with a ladle-shaped spoon that lifted the mud into containers onboard the vessel.

Ice boat at work, Conduit Colliery
The ice boat was common to all canal undertakings as an essential part of their maintenance fleet. Ice stopped navigation in winter and canal companies were compelled to keep the waterway free, wherever possible, or face loss of trade. The method usually adopted was the ice boat which was made specifically for the task. Despite the large number of factories and works that discharged warm water on the core central area of the BCN, the windswept wastes of the Cannock Chase coalfield were prone to freezing in cold weather and several BCN ice boats were deployed in this district. Each was made to the same small and narrow design comprising wood reinforced with iron. They broke the ice through the combined action of groups of men aboard rocking from side to side and a team of horses on the towpath forcing the craft forward. The view above shows an ice boat in action near Conduit Colliery. The date would be about 1920. (*Birmingham Public Libraries, Local Studies Department*)

Fan boat, Ten Score Bridge
The fan boat is perhaps one of the most unusual contraptions used on the BCN. It utilised a steam engine to drive a paddle wheel placed at the fore end of the vessel. The boat was adapted for maintenance purposes where it was used to draw water from a section of the canal. Stop planks were inserted at one end of the section, whilst the boat was placed in a bridge hole at the other end. The steam engine drove the fan wheel, which rotated to draw water from the pound. In this view a fan boat is seen on the BCN at a place believed to be Ten Score Bridge, near Bilston Steelworks. (*Wolverhampton Public Libraries*)

92

Six

Working on the Canals

Canals served midlands industry for 200 years. These lines of artificial communication were first opened to Birmingham in 1769 and gradually grew in number until a network of waterways was established across the town. The BCN was linked to other local waterways which in turn joined with others that formed part of the system of inland navigation that linked London and the South with the Midlands, North East and the North West. Construction, operation and trade brought many people to work on the canals. They came from a wide range of backgrounds and places.

The first to be associated with any canal enterprise were promoters – the bankers, solicitors and clerks who put the scheme together. It was they who saw the opportunity to make the waterway and then formed the company to build it. An engineer and surveyor were then approached to investigate the lie of the land and devise a route. Once a viable scheme was formed, investors were approached to put money into the venture. Everything at this stage was confined to the offices of lawyers and accountants. A plan was drawn up and an application to Parliament made. Objections from landowners and other interested parties were taken into consideration and subject to these objections, approval for the Act authorising the canal was given. The next stage was to raise enough capital to begin the work. Once this was done contracts for the construction were advertised in the local papers.

Whenever a canal was built the first group of people to come on site were the contractors and labourers commonly known as the navvies. These were a semi-nomadic group of people who moved from job to job as needed. They included the unskilled labourers who with simple tools dug out the waterway and made the towpaths, embankments, cuttings and tunnels. Working with this crowd were the stonemasons, bricklayers and carpenters. These were the people who made the bridges, houses, locks and toll offices. There were also the contractors who planted the hedges and made the fences. Once the water was let into the navigation trade could commence. The canal companies were then entitled to charge tolls and rents to recoup the shareholders' investment. Frequently sections of canal were opened before the whole line was complete. When the route was finished, that was generally the limit of operation. Some canals, such as the Birmingham Canal Navigations continued to add extra mileage to their existing network.

Trade varied from canal to canal. Midland industry was dependent on coal, which was mined locally in the Black Country, on Cannock Chase, and throughout the Leicestershire and Warwickshire coalfields. Coal, ironstone, limestone, sand and road stone were carried by narrow boats across the Midland canal system. The common boats used in this traffic were the joey boats. The boatmen who worked them comprised a crew of two: one to steer the boat, the other the drive the horse and work the locks. These vessels worked relatively short distances and their crew lived on land. Theirs was a very different life from those whose working life was often perpetually afloat

The long-distance trade inevitably meant that boat crews were away from their home depot for days at a time. During each journey the boat cabin became home to the crew. In the early years of canal carriage, long-distance boats included the two major groups that were the fly boats and the stage boats. Fly boat crews worked in teams of two when one team slept as the other worked the boat. The slower stage boat travelled shorter distances but called at all wharves and like the fly boat was often away from the home base for a number of days.

With the establishment of a national railway network after 1850, the use of the fly and stage boat declined, but cabin boat trade was adapted to handle specific contract cargos. These boats went from contract to contract and were manned by crews who made the boat cabin their permanent home. These were the family boats. The head of the family was the captain and was assisted by the rest of the family. The wife had probably the hardest task. She cooked, looked after the children as well as often steering the boat.

The main mode of propulsion for canal craft was the horse. Each horse required care and attention. Canalside stables that provided overnight accommodation for the horses had to be manned. The harness and gearing had to be purchased and maintained. The blacksmith provided the shoes and the farrier was employed to fit them and look after the health of the animal.

Another aspect of the canal was the company workforce. Each canal company employed people to collect tolls, wharf dues and rents. Clerks were employed in the offices to process correspondence, accounts and deal with company records. They also had a group of people responsible for maintenance. The toll collector was often the main contact between the boatmen and the canal company. Their role was to check the passing boats with the gauge stick and verify their cargo. They collected the tolls for the journey made and issued a ticket as a receipt.

Water supply was integral to canal operation and staff were needed to ensure a steady and continued flow. Many companies used steam engines to pump water into the canal or storage reservoirs. Engineers were needed to work the engines and stokers to fire the boilers. Maintenance staff was used to repair the waterway. Locks and bridges had a finite life and required attention from time to time. Lock walls, in particular, were taken down and replaced when water got in behind the brickwork or masonry. Silt and weeds frequently clogged waterways and this had to be removed to maintain navigation. This job fell to the dredger, which labourers worked often spooning out foul smelling detritus into a mud boat.

In the winter, canals were often blocked by ice and the company got out its iceboats to keep a clear passage. These unique craft were sturdy built and were treated roughly. A team on men manned the boat rocking it from side to side as horses on the bank forced the boat through the ice.

Private wharves were the responsibility of the wharfinger, who managed the wharf collecting dues for warehouse storage, crane use and carriage rates. Commercial carriers operated from both public and private wharves and operated a fleet of boats. Before the establishment of a national railway network these wharves served as waterside 'goods stations' and employed clerks, wharf porters and stablemen. Even after the public railways were constructed canal wharves still retained an important function for the carriage of goods. Colliery, limestone and furnace wharves commonly employed their own loaders, who were used to load the boats. Working in the open air, these men were a hardy breed exposed to all nature might throw at them.

The care of welfare of the boating population was initially ignored, but from 1840 there was a growing concern for their spiritual needs. Canalside missions were established to hold services for the boatmen and arrangements for education of the children was also arranged. These missions were usually located at places were boatmen congregated, especially at lock flights where they had long waits for their turn at the lock.

Canals therefore provided employment for a wide variety of trades and professions. During the last fifty years commercial traffic has been considerably reduced. The boatmen today are boaters who use the waterways for leisure use and there still a need for maintenance and repair and a constant demand for re-opening disued waterways to serve the boaters' needs. It is a very different waterway today than it was in time of the working boat, but that is down to progress!

Nineteenth-Century Social Developments

The Victorian era saw the greatest development of local canalside industry. There was also a corresponding increase in concern for workers welfare. Boatmen's missions were established to look after religious needs, whilst living conditions within the boat cabin came to be rigidly inspected. Canal boat inspection became the responsibility of certain local authorities following the Canal Boat Act of 1877. Birmingham, Brierley Hill and Wolverhampton were given the right to inspect and register canal boats on the BCN. Inspectors attached to the Heath and Sanitary Departments were appointed to enforce the requirements of the Act. A second Act in 1884 increased the powers of inspection and gave all local authorities powers to inspect boats. The task of registration generally remained with the original inspection authorities.

Wolverhampton Sanitary Committee appointed two inspectors – Samuel Blanton and George Thomas – on 14 October 1878, who set about the task of visiting all the boats that passed through Wolverhampton on the BCN and Staffordshire & Worcestershire Canal. Each boat was given a registration number, which had to be painted on the boat cabin. Registration was only given when the boat complied with the Act. There were rules concerning air space with the cabin, number of people sleeping there, state of cabin, state of repair, paintwork and provision of a suitable water can. All cabin boat owners were required to register their boats within a time limit and once that had passed owners might be fined.

According to the *Birmingham Daily Post* (2 February 1884), Elijah Banner, of Star Ironworks, Wednesfield Heath, was fined 5s and costs for having an unregistered boat on the Birmingham Canal. James Sandbach, the steerer, was also summoned and ordered to pay 4s costs.

Samuel Blanton took his boat inspection role very seriously, which is evident in the Wolverhampton Sanitary Committee minutes. The following information has been extracted from a report by Samuel Blanton made to the Wolverhampton Sanitary Committee on 13 September 1881:

> Near Gasworks. *Ashby*, Shropshire Union boat No.207, registered Chester No.29 for 3 people or man, wife and two children. In the occupation of Absolom Hampton with wife, boy (7), boy (6), girl (4,) boy (2) and baby (6 months). Hampton told me he had only two of his children with him on this voyage and that the Company was to provide him with a two-cabin boat. I have seen Mr Sedgewick and am informed that this is the case.

> *Morton*, Shropshire Union boat No.285, registered Chester – Francis Goode, wife and Alfred Whalley, aged over 14 yrs. No ventilated screen to divide cross and side beds.

> At Bottom Lock. *Rose*, owner – Fellows, Morton & Co., registered Wolverhampton No.137. Occupied by Joseph Harker, wife, daughter (over 14) – she should not be on the boat. Mr Barnes seen and girls should not go on boat.

> At Bottom Lock. *Queen Victoria*, owner – Earl Granville of Etruria Ironworks, master John Downes, in the charge of Joseph Marston and Thomas Downes. Boat <u>not registered</u> to meet requirements of Act. Fixed cross bed. No water vessels. Boat loaded with pig iron. Men said it was an odd journey.

Brothers, owner – Mary Kirkham, master – Joseph Preese, registered at Kiddermister and had no certificate. Boat was dirty and had no water vessel.

Selina, owner – George Archer of Millfields, master – David Sheldon, registered No.109 at Stoke. Did not have certificates with him.

Near Dunstall Meadows. *Ralph*, registered at Wolverhampton No.87, owner – William Foster, occupied by Frank Sanders, wife and Samuel Turner. No ventilated screen

No.4. Belongs to Isaac Slater Junior, Ilkeston, Derbyshire. Does not meet regulations – has a fixed cross bed.

Others inspected that day: *Excelsior* was seen near the Shropshire Union Wharf (SU No.307) and the *Martha & Elizabeth*, near Top Lock, belonging to Joseph Whitehouse, West Bromwich, registered at Rugeley.

Canal boat inspection fulfilled other roles. Boat people found to be carrying infectious diseases such typhoid, scarlet fever and diphtheria were removed to hospital and the boat disinfected. Inspectors were also concerned about the education of boat children. The following is an extract from a circular sent to all health authorities during October 1894:

Extract of Report of Commission of Council on Education 1893-1894
Observations on the Working of Scheme for Education
under Canal Boats Act 1877 and 1884

In the present and imperfect and inoperative state of law regarding educating the migratory classes, our first and principal efforts have been not towards educating the children, but on getting such of them as are still on boats removed to houses on shore where they can be dealt with by the school authority in the usual way along with other children, and failing that, then to do the best we can with those whose parents have no home but the boat cabin. Year by year they are becoming reduced in number, and though it may be long before children of school age are entirely removed from the canal boats, still as if as great success attends the efforts of the future as it has done in the past then it will be a subject for congratulation that this section of the community – the canal boat population – does not need the special attention that has been necessary to bestow upon it of late years so as to get its children under the influence of elementary education.

With children living on boats there must always be a certain amount of difficulty in seasonal attendance at school, chiefly owing to the shortness of time that a boat remains at any one given place and some times owing to the disinclination of the teachers to admit children who are not permanently residing in the district. Some authorities however state that during last year they experienced no difficulty in obtaining an average attendance at school of said children. In many districts, the Canal Boat Inspectors, when they meet a child of school age on board may beat immediate communication regarding item with the school authorities of the place to which the boat is registered.

Notwithstanding the dislocation of trade caused by the coal strike of 1893, which told severely upon the earnings of the canal boatmen, many of their boats have lain idle for months together, it is gratifying to notice that they have not had recourse, unless in very exceptional cases, to the abandoning of their homes or the re-introduction of their children to the boats.

Samuel Blanton became the sole inspector of boats for Wolverhampton and remained in this post until his death in 1898. The Health Committee had absorbed the Sanitary Department by this time. Their minutes dated 13 September 1898 make the following remark:

> The Health Committee record with regret and sadness of the death of S. Blanton, late inspector of Nuisance and also under the Canal Boats Act for the Borough. During his office connection with the Corporation extended over a period of 27 years. Mr Blanton rendered efficient and self-denying service and conscientiously ably discharged the important duties required of him. This Committee desire to express to members of his family their sympathy with the bereaved.

Boatmen's Missions

Canal people were not the ungodly lot that some writers have made them out to be. Many followed either the conformist or non-conformist religions. They married in church and had their children baptised. The frequent nomadic existence often meant that religious devotion was conducted at churches along the way. Boating families however had their favourite churches to visit as baptism records show.

Missions for boatpeople came to be established at canalside locations during the 1840s. An early mission (whose owner is not known) was erected beside the top lock at Farmer's Bridge, Birmingham, about this time. Later missions came to be built by two groups. One was the Incorporated Seamen & Boatmen's Friend Society, the other was the Church of England Diocese of Lichfield.

The Diocese of Lichfield operated a floating barge mission near Can Lane Wharf, Wolverhampton, which by 1882 had fallen into disrepair. A strip of land between Littles Lane and the Top Lock Cottages was then acquired and a new permanent boatmen's mission erected there. This building, which was completed during 1884, became known as the Barge Mission and was looked after by the clergy of St Mary's Parish. A second mission building was completed for the Lichfield Diocesan Barge Mission at Tipton between 1892 and 1893.

The Seamen & Boatmen's Friend Society rented rooms on Worcester Wharf, Birmingham, that they used as a Bethel Chapel from about 1860. Attendances may not have been high but they improved after Richard Cusworth was appointed Superintendent of the Birmingham Mission, in 1872. Cusworth, who had previously been involved with missionary work in India, replaced the Reverend James Pilkington at the Worcester Wharf Chapel. Richard Cusworth had both drive and ability, and it was through his efforts that a larger congregation was built up. Worcester Wharf had been established by the Worcester & Birmingham Canal Co., but was now owned by the Sharpness New Docks and the Gloucester & Birmingham Navigation Co. It comprised a mixture of carriers' depots, corn warehouses and timber yards. The Bethel Chapel was situated in their midst beside the road which ran up onto Worcester Wharf from Wharf Street.

New railway works threatened the future existence of Worcester Wharf Mission. The land where the Bethel Chapel stood was needed for the new Central Goods Station. In March 1877, the Seamen & Boatmen's Friend Society applied to the Canal Company for a new site on Worcester Wharf to build a Bethel School. The Canal Company asked manager W.D. George to find out how many children might attend this school. George later reported that no more than fifteen boat children would be of an age to attend the school. The Canal Company decided that 'it would not be desirable to erect a school on Worcester Wharf' but agreed to investigate the matter of a site for reading rooms. The future of the Birmingham Mission remained in doubt, but through a gift of £2,000 from Miss Ryland, the Seamen & Boatmen's Friend Society were able to secure enough funds build a new chapel on another part of the Worcester Wharf.

The new Boatmen's Mission Hall, designed by Osborn & Reading, was opened 17 March, 1879. It was a tall three storied red brick building, which straddled a narrow thoroughfare called the Gullet. On the ground floor were separate coffee rooms for the men and women, lavatories, a drying room and a kitchen where boatmen could cook their food. On the floor above was a lofty hall that could hold over 150 people and above that were bedrooms for the caretaker.

Unfortunately, the new Boatman's Chapel had a brief existence. Birmingham Borough Council decided, in 1882, to make road improvements and extend Holliday Street through to Wharf Street by removing the Gullet and demolishing any buildings that stood in the path of the works. Miss Ryland's committee looked for new premises. Negotiation went on with Birmingham Council, the Canal Company and the Midland Railway. In 1884 the Midland Railway provided a new site for the mission, which was at the corner of Bridge Street and Wharf Street close to both the Worcester & Birmingham Canal and BCN properties. The Bridge Street Mission was completed by 1885. It was of similar design and had similar accommodation to the 1879 version. The Bridge Street Mission was opened in time for the autumn meeting of the Seamen & Boatmen's Friend Society, which was attended by delegates from all over the country. Special thanks were given to Miss Ryland for establishing the new hall in Birmingham.

Reverend Cusworth continued his ministry to the boat people and education for boat children. He constantly strove to increase the efforts of his team of ministers to raise funds for new missions and other works. Through them was funded the Hednesford and Walsall missions as well as a group of shelters for boat horses. They conducted summer time open-air services for boatmen at the canalside and visited boats handing out literature and religious texts. Theirs was necessary work as was exemplified by their chairman, J.D. Goodman's, message, read out at the annual meeting at Worcester Wharf in March 1884:

> The life of the boatman was a very peculiar one, and the public hardly realised how much they were indebted to this body of men, who conveyed their goods from place to place, and who had to endure a great many hardships in carrying on their necessary work. [Goodman] thoroughly sympathised with them in the difficulties with which they had to contend, and if it was in [his] power to assist them at any time he would be pleased to do so. [He] trusted that employers would do something in establishing coffee-houses in the immediate vicinity of the canals, to promote the temperance amongst the boatmen, which was so desirable, not only in the interests of the public, but also for their own social welfare.

The Boatmen's Hall and Coffee Room, Hednesford, Staffordshire.

THE Boatmen's Hall, Hednesford (a sketch of which is given above) was erected by the Society at a cost of £650, and was opened on Friday, June 21st, 1885, by the late Sir Richard Moon, Bart. It is erected on land kindly leased to the Society by Messrs. P. Williams and Sons, of Wednesbury Oak Works, and comprises Mission Room and Caretaker's Apartments, occupied by the Missionary in charge.

A sketch of the Boatmen's Hall, Hednesford, Staffordshire, taken from the Annual Report (Midland District) of the Incorporated Seamen & Boatmen's Friend Society, March 1901.

George Robert Jebb

George Robert Jebb had a distinguished career as a waterways engineer, which spanned fifty years. Few have equalled this achievement and it is a credit to the man that he spent so much time in this service.

He was born on 30 November 1838 at Baschurch, in Shropshire, the son of John and Martha Jebb, and was christened at the parish church on 26 December, 1838. George trained as an engineer under the tutelage of Alexander Mackintosh from 1854 to 1858. Mackintosh was then in charge of the Chester lines of the GWR. In 1859 he received his first appointment as resident engineer on the Bryn-y-Owen Railway and the Wrexham and Minera Railway. From 1862 to 1869 he was engaged on similar work for the GWR, including the Minera Railway extension. In 1863 he went to Galicia and planned the course of the twenty-mile-long Lemberg to Czernowitz Railway. Jebb might have continued to work exclusively in railway engineering but, in 1869, accepted the post of chief engineer to the Shropshire Union Railways & Canal Co. It was a post that was to test his skills to the limit. The Shropshire Union, which had been leased to the London & North Western Railway in 1847, had some twenty-nine miles of public railway, opened in 1849, which extended from Stafford to Wellington. They had joint running powers on the GWR line from Wellington to Shrewsbury and had independent goods sidings in Shrewsbury.

The engineering for all this became the responsibility of George Jebb. It was a considerable duty, for this was a time of change. Railway transport was increasing, whilst canal transport was in decline. Limited funds were consequently available for canal maintenance from the LNWR purse. Yet Jebb seemed to have the knack to get the money for his projects and he managed to keep the canals in good order. In fact, he improved them. By 1914 the 200-plus miles of the Shropshire Union Canal were said to be in better condition than they had ever been before. Amongst his achievements for this company was that he was responsible for the construction of deep-water docks and warehouses at Ellesmere Port.

In 1875 George Jebb was also appointed chief engineer to the BCN, which then had about 160 miles of waterway. By this date the BCN was controlled by the LNWR, and the people at Euston might have influenced Jebb's appointment. It was to prove as beneficial for the BCN as it was for the Shropshire Union. During the time Jebb held the post of chief engineer to the BCN (1875-1912). He improved the waterway using LNWR funds. Large sums were spent on making the canal watertight, increasing the carrying capacity, widening the waterway, walling towing paths, increasing reservoir capacity and substituting new and economical pumping plant for others that were now old fashioned.

His work for the BCN appears in many archive sources and is valuable aid to historians researching this canal. They include maps and drawings, reports and written documents. His maps of the BCN are particularly useful as they are sufficiently detailed to show every company wharf and level. Jebb designed the Parkhead and Smethwick engine houses. These two new pumping plants were to have a significant effect on the canal water supply. They are events for which George Jebb deserves full credit.

The pumping plant at Parkhead employed modern pumping engines which were able to re-circulate water between the busiest traffic routes, that is the 440 ft (Level Pound), 453ft (Birmingham) and 473ft (Wolverhampton). These engines commenced pumping in 1891. The Brasshouse Lane pumping plant at Smethwick, which re-circulated water between the 453ft and 473ft levels, followed them about a year later. It replaced the old pumping engines located in Bridge Street.

Jebb acted as consulting engineer and attended several important enquiries into canal affairs, despite being actively engaged in canal maintenance and improvement over a long period. When apart from his duties in the public view, Jebb was a very private individual and frequently declined to be interviewed. He was appointed a member of the Council for the Institute of Civil Engineers in 1902 and was Vice President of that society between 1912 and 1915. Jebb resigned from the CICE when he was nominated for the office of President in 1915. George Jebb, was evidently a person who shied away from publicity and was a man of definite views in this respect. He appears to have undervalued his own personal achievements and even till his death rarely talked about his life or family. Jebb lived in Shrewsbury when he first undertook his BCN contracts, but later had a house beside the Newton Road in Great Barr. In full retirement he moved to Bucklebury Common, near Reading, where he died, on 16 February 1927.

The tar boat Erne

Gaily painted boats were sometimes the public perception of life on canals. The reality was very different. Whole families contributed to the working of a boat, often for a single wage paid to the head of the family. Boats had to be worked day-in day-out, whatever the weather. Payment was usually for the trip so if the boat was delayed through ice or stoppages, there was no pay. Yet for those who worked the boats it was their accustomed way of life and had been for generations. Son followed father as father had followed grandfather into the boating trade. Boys and girls grew up on the boats, worked on the boats, got married on the boats and lived their whole life through in what was a close-knit community. Family relationships were complex as most boat people were related to each other in some fashion. In this picture the Thomas Clayton butty *Erne* is seen with mother on the tiller and two children looking out from the back of the boat. (*Boat Museum, Ellesmere Port*)

The tar boat Tiber

The tar boat *Tiber* is seen approaching Gorsebrook Viaduct on the Wolverhampton Flight. Painted with Thomas Clayton's name, this boat had been purchased by them second hand from Midland Tar Distillers in 1938. Smoke billows from the chimney as the stove below endeavors to keep the cabin warm on what appears to be a cold day. A mug and cup rest on the cabin roof as the woman steers the butty towards the next lock. The buckby can rests on the roof behind the chimney. Cans such as these held the drinking water for those on board. Many boaters today choose to have these cans to adorn their cabin roof even though they may had a perfectly adequate water system within their boat. (*Boat Museum, Ellesmere Port*)

Allan Stevens (opposite)

Allan 'Caggy' Stevens spent his working life on the canals. He assisted his father bringing loads of coal from the Cannock Chase Mines to F.W Ratcliffe & Co. of Tipton. Allan Stevens was born in 1918 and worked for his father from the age of fourteen years. He drove a horse during these early times, but was paid little until he was eighteen years old. Caggy later set up in business on his own account to carry all sorts of goods. His main occupation remained, however, the carriage of coal. Stevens served coal yards, factories, ironworks and power stations in his time, but with the decline of the coal trade worked as a general canal contractor, taking whatever job was available. For one period he was in partnership with Ken Keay and together they owned two tugs and sixteen boats. Caggy, at this time operated from a depot a Whimsey Bridge, Oldbury, whilst Ken operated from Birchills. Their partnership was eventually dissolved and Caggy went back to work for his own account. In 1978 he took over a collection of disused wharves at Tipton, which became his new depot. He remained there until his death. With his passing went the last of the true BCN canal carriers.

Caggy Stevens and horse boat Caro
(above)
Caggy Stevens with horse and the joey
boat *Caro*. The *Caro* had formerly
belonged to Ernest Thomas and had
been used by him to take coal from
Cannock Chase to the GEC at
Witton. (*Geoff Bennet*)

Caggy Stevens with horse (right)
Caggy Stevens is seen here with his
boat horse. The horse is wearing a
typical harness bedecked with brasses,
whilst feeding from the traditional
nose tin. (*Geoff Bennet*)

Tar Boats Dane *and* Gipping *at Clayton's Yard, Oldbury*

Canals were a way of life for some families. The waterways provided employment and the boat cabins house and home. Mr Dan Jinks and family are seen sitting on the cabins of two tar boats moored at Thomas Clayton's dock at Oldbury. The tar boats were amongst the last family working boats to be used on the BCN. The woman and girl are sitting on the cabin of the motorboat *Dane* that the Claytons purchased second-hand from the Severn & Canal Carrying Co. in 1950. Mr and Mrs Jinks are seated beside the cabin of the butty *Gipping*, which was added to the Clayton fleet in 1926. (*Edward Paget Tomlinson Collection*)

Seven

Modern Times and Modern Developments

Commercial traffic on the BCN declined after 1920 as more and more traffic was switched to the roads or railways. The gradual decline escalated after 1950 and parts of the system were abandoned. Some sixty miles of navigation was officially closed to traffic. Included in the closures were the line of locks through Ogley Hay and Lichfield, portions of the Old Main Line from Bradley to Tipton, the Bradley Lock flight and the Tipton to Toll End communication.

Some traffic continued on the remaining 100-plus miles of navigation but, with each passing year, there were less and less commercial boat movements. The single most destructive factor was the hard winter of 1962-1963 where the canal was frozen for weeks. Ice breakers tried to keep the traffic moving from the collieries, but the waterway quickly froze. Eventually there was no water left in some parts and both loaded and empty narrow boats lay stranded in an icy white wilderness.

British Waterways revenue figures for 1964 reveal that the bulk of revenue was from sales of water and parts of the BCN even made a small profit that year. Consideration was given to reducing many of the canals to water channels to reduce expenditure. It was a proposal vigorously opposed by the boaters who were beginning to have a greater say in waterways affairs. The boaters were a group of people who owned their own craft and travelled along the inland navigation for pleasure. Their numbers began to swell after 1950 and, through their efforts, certain canals remained open. The BCN was still an industrial waterway, but this did not deter some intrepid boaters to navigate it on a regular basis. Routes such as the Birmingham & Fazeley Canal were particularly popular as this canal principally passed through a rural landscape. Several of the BCN boatyards also stayed in business building and repairing pleasure craft as well as converting some of the older working boats for leisure use.

British Waterways had split the BCN into two administrative districts and made the core BCN in the Black Country and Cannock Chase separate from the Birmingham & Fazeley Canal. In 1968 came a further distinction that labelled certain waterways as Cruiseways and others as Remainder Waterways. A large chunk of the BCN became a Remainder Waterway and suffered through lack of investment accordingly.

The canalside infrastructure started to change. Cottages were demolished; warehouses were left to fall into decay and property was either sold off of let at a cheap rent. Property values were somewhat lower for those whose houses backed onto the 'cut'. The towpaths became 'unofficial' public footpaths and the canal a haunt for fishermen. Weeds began to clog up the navigation and would have succeeded were it not for the passing of the pleasure boats.

Then came the change. Waterside property was deemed desirable and investors started to see the value of canalside property. This is most noticeable in Birmingham where regeneration has completely transformed the canalside scene. The process began around Gas Street Basin and has spread out along the New Main Line and loops towards Ladywood. It is also progressing along the Birmingham & Fazeley and Digbeth branches. Parts have also been transformed at Brierley Hill, Walsall and Wednesbury. The next target for the developers is the Horseleyfield district at Wolverhampton where surviving structures of our industrial heritage are in danger of being lost.

Against this changing backdrop is an increased awareness by the waterways authorities to improve the navigation and provide better facilities for the boaters, hire boaters, walkers, cyclists and fishermen. Boating traffic has seen a considerable increase since 1980 and the prospect of investment in restoring disused navigations promises to increase traffic on the local canals. Schemes to re-open Lapal Tunnel on the Dudley Canal (closed since 1917) and the seven-mile link from Ogley through Lichfield to Coventry Canal are ambitious projects yet are now within the realms of being done. The Lichfield Canal project has a particularly active group who are seemingly defying the odds and are systemically getting the line ready for restoration.

Dunstall Park Bridge (below)
Dunstall Park Bridge, Wolverhampton Locks, is quite evidently in a rural setting even though quite close to the industrial conurbation. In its isolated location there has been less opportunity for change and this bridge is probably an early example of BCN bridge making and may even date from 1772 when the canal was opened to this point.

Wolverhampton Locks
The Wolverhampton Lock flight comprises twenty-one locks, which descend through a former industrial district that once included gasworks, railway sidings, a locomotive coaling plant and a manure works. One of the few remaining industrial features is the refuse depot that lines the canal there. The canal towpath has been considerably improved since the days of the working boat.

Huddlesford Junction, 1998
Huddlesford Junction was created in 1797 when the Wyrley & Essington Canal Co. opened a communication with the Coventry Canal near Whittington. In this photograph the view is along the Coventry Canal and the Wyrley & Essington Canal is seen to join from the right. The roving bridge was constructed to carry the towpath over onto the towpath for the Wyrley & Essington Canal. The junction buildings belonged to the Coventry Canal Co. and served as canal house and toll cottage. They are now the headquarters for the boat club who use the stub of the Wyrley & Essington Canal that is still in water as residential moorings.

Darnford Lane Lift Bridge
The Lichfield & Hatherton Trust was formed by a group of volunteers who got together to restore a disused part of the Wyrley & Essington Canal – the Hatherton Branch Canal – and to make a new waterway that joined the Hatherton branch with the Cannock Extension Canal at Grove Colliery Basin. Their plan being to open new navigable links that joined the BCN, Coventry Canal and the Staffordshire & Worcestershire Canal and open up new cruising routes for boaters. Progress is steadily being made with the Lichfield Canal that formed the disused section of the Wyrley & Essington Canal from Ogley Hay to Huddlesford. Sections are steadily being restored. This 1998 view is of the part between lock 30 and Darnford Lane, where the course has been altered and the bank piled. A lift bridge has been installed as part of the improvements being made. This lift bridge had been first installed by British Waterways on the Peak Forest Canal, near Whalley Bridge, but had become redundant through road improvements there. The bridge was then purchased by the Chesterfield Canal Society, who stored it for a number of years before handing it over to the Lichfield & Hatherton Trust. Darnford Lane Lift Bridge is therefore a new feature for the waterway. Previously swing bridges had existed on the Wyrley & Essington Canal, although there was a lift bridge near the end of the Wyrley Bank Canal.

Lodge Farm Reservoir, 1976 (opposite top)
Lodge Farm Reservoir as seen through the trees. Lodge Farm Reservoir was constructed between 1835 and 1838 to supply water to the Dudley Canal. It was constructed on the bed of the original route of the waterway, which was diverted under the hillside through the short Brewin's Tunnel. Lodge Farm was a storage reservoir and at times of heavy rainfall could extract water out of the canal using a steam powered scoop wheel installed in 1840. Water was let out into the canal when needed through sluices near Brewin's Tunnel. A cottage was built here presumably for the use of the sluice keeper, the roof of which can be seen in the right of the picture. Brewin's Tunnel was opened out in 1858 as part canal improvement work made by the BCN to the line of the Dudley Canal.

Water-skiing, Lodge Farm Reservoir (opposite middle)
Lodge Farm Reservoir was sold by British Waterways to Dudley Council in 1966, who developed the leisure side there. This evening shot for 1978 shows water-skiing in action; there is now a sailing club established there as well.

Horseleyfields, 2001 (opposite below)
The Horseleyfields area of Wolverhampton still retains many industrial features even though their days may be numbered. On one cold December day in 2001 the view along the BCN looking under the Horseleyfields towards Walsall Street Bridge was typically industrial. Even a side bridge remains intact covering the entrance to a long disused basin.

Oozells Loop looking towards Morris's Rolling Mills
Birmingham was a principal producer of rolled non-ferrous metals and had works placed all round the city engaged in this trade. Such works relied on the canal for coal to drive their steam-powered rolling mills and heat the annealing furnaces, but with change over to electric mills and furnaces, the need for coal by boat was discontinued. Firms such as W. Morris, however, retain their canalside location and form an industrial backdrop for the waterway here.

Walsall Town Arm, 1979 (opposite top)
When the CEGB decided to finally abandon canal coal traffic in 1967. The boats fleet used in this trade were left abandoned alongside the waterway or pushed into basins or arms. Walsall Town Arm accumulated its share, one of which No.219, is seen on the side of the canal in 1979. Some boats were eventually taken away, but at least one remained at the end of the Town Arm until the mid-1990s. (*Walsall Local Studies Centre*)

Walsall Canal Birchills Locks, 1969 (opposite below)
The view, as seen from the third lock looking towards Birchills Street Bridge, was a typical industrial scene of the period. The buildings on the right formed part of an iron foundry that belonged to T.H Mold & Son. (*Walsall Local Studies Centre*)

Trip Boat Jericho *on Oozells Loop* (next page)
The trip boat *Jericho* passes the PPG paint factory as part of the regular run from the ICC that goes round by way of the Oozells and Icknield Port Loops.

Gas Street Basin, 1979
Gas Street Basin, before the general redevelopment of the area took place. Gas Street formed the end of the BCN when the Old Wharf was closed and filled in. With the decline of canal carrying, Gas Street remained a haven for canal boats. It was a hidden world lying behind the buildings that fronted Broad Street. Here, in the 1960s and 1970s, boaters would take advantage of the disused wharves for residential moorings.

GEC Power Station, Birmingham & Fazeley Canal, 1990
The view south along the Tame Valley Canal from Deakins Avenue Bridge overlooks the bottom lock. The buildings foundations on the right were formerly part of the pumping station that was used to re-circulate water to the top of the locks. Beside the bottom lock two canal cottages can be seen, whilst behind this group is the GEC works power station and telpher. This power station once received regular consignments of coal by boat.

Iron Bridge over Causeway Green Arm
The date plate of the iron bridge had been torn off by the time this picture was taken in 1983, but probably read 1858, the year the canal was completed.

Causeway Green Arm
A six-coach diesel multiple unit train travels along the railway embankment towards Rowley Regis Station in 1983. In the foreground, the dry bed of the Causeway Green Arm is seen to head towards this embankment. The Causeway Green Arm was a short branch completed to link the Titford Canal with various brickworks and collieries located near Causeway Green. The railway, finished in 1867, originally crossed the end of the canal branch by a bridge. A few yards beyond this bridge was Cakemore Wharf and brickyard. Colliery loading wharves also existed near the end of the branch for the tramway that brought coal down from Rowley Station Colliery to the canal. Parts of the Arm were abandoned from 1954, but the dry bed remained for all to see until the late 1990s.

Dudley No.2 Canal at the Saltwells looking towards the Two-Lock Line
The Saltwells takes its name from the mineral springs there, but was better known as mining area. This 1978 photograph shows the view from High Bridge looking towards Brierley Hill, before the steelworks there was closed. The course of the Dudley Canal can be followed as it curves around the hillside towards Two-Lock Line Junction.

Two-Lock Line Towpath Bridge
From 1858, the Two-Lock Line was considered to be part of the main Dudley Canal. This short piece of connecting waterway had shortened the distance between Netherton and Brierley Hill and reduced the route via Blowers Green to secondary status. This photograph shows the towpath bridge, in 1990, which spanned the entrance to the Two-Lock Line. Mining subsidence finally lead to the closure of the Two-Lock Line. The nearby toll office was also closed and eventually demolished. The main route for the Dudley Canal then reverted to that via Blowers Green.

Towpath Bridge Swan Village Interchange Basin

In recent years canal regeneration has received finance for a range of schemes, but not all have favoured the boaters. The construction of the Black Country Spine Road promised to cut the navigable link to a rarely used section of the BCN, which was known as the Ridgacre Canal, but also included a section of the Balls Hill Branch and Swan Village Railway Interchange Basin. The new road was to pass across the canal almost of the level and eliminate the navigable channel. Despite objections from canal enthusiasts and boaters, no provision was made for navigation when the road was constructed. In this 1998 photograph the view is along the now isolated Interchange Basin looking under the footbridge to a piece of the Balls Hill branch. Separated from these waters is the Ridgacre branch whilst across the Spine Road is the truncated end of the Balls Hill branch that is still linked to the main BCN system. The Ridgacre pub was not built at the time these canal alterations were made; had it been there the boaters and enthusiasts might have had a more forceful argument to retain the right of navigation. However, whilst the boaters now lose out on travelling along a short piece of BCN waterway, the fishermen and walkers gain some benefit. The towpath side has been refurbished and stages installed for the fishermen to use.

The Black Country Museum and Dudley Tunnel

For those interested in industrial archaeology, the Dudley Canal Tunnel is both accessible and provides visible evidence of the industrial past. It has a complicated history associated with the mining of limestone and coal, and some parts predate the 1792 tunnel, which forms the main connection between the BCN and old Dudley Canal. The original tunnel dates from about 1778 and was formed as a private canal by Lord Ward. Lord Ward was associated with a number of private cuts and waterways, which include the Foxyards and Pensnett Canals. The private canal at Tipton was his first and was originally made in 1776 to the Tipton Colliery. A branch was formed from this private cut about 1778 to pass under the hillside to get the limestone. Gradually a network of subterranean canals developed through the limestone rock. Small boats, not unlike the starvationers of the Worsley coalmines, near Manchester, plied the narrow channels bringing stone out from the underground man made caverns. With the passing of the second Dudley Canal Act in 1785, work started on the main tunnel, which was over 2900yds long (2942yds to Castle Mill basin). This photograph shows the Dudley Canal approach to the Tipton Portal of Dudley Canal Tunnel as seen from Birmingham Road Bridge during the late 1970s. It shows the Black Country Museum during the early stages of developments and the restoration work done at this time by the Dudley Canal Trust.

Basin Black Country Museum, 1984
On one part of the extensive Black Country Museum site is the restored canal arm and basin that served the Earl of Dudley's new limestone kilns. This stretch of waterway was utilised as moorings for various heritage craft and parts of the banks were adapted as boatyards for traditional boat repair skills to be carried out. In this photograph the view is across the basin looking towards the rolling mill site.

IWA Rally, Titford Pools
Titford Pools are the oldest surviving reservoir that still supplies water to the BCN network. The original reservoir, made between 1773 and 1774, fed water into Smethwick Level at Spon Lane. Thomas Telford changed the water supply by redirecting Titford water via a new feeder to Edgbaston Reservoir made between 1826 and 1830. Further changes to the reservoir were made in 1836 and 1837 when the Titford Canal was constructed to what became the highest navigable level on the BCN (511ft). The making of the Titford Canal enabled boats to work up to the reservoir and this navigable link has remained. Titford Locks briefly fell into disuse before restoration in 1973 and 1974. In this view a boater is seen to take his ease beside his boat at the 1976 IWA Boat Rally.

Reliving the past at IWE Rally, NIA, 2000
The first Inland Waterways Exhibition was held at Birmingham's National Indoor Arena in 2000. The many working boats that attended this event were moored at Cambrian Wharf. Each craft joined a cavalcade of boats that passed along the canal beside the NIA, whilst canal historian Laurence Hogg narrated their respective histories.

Sherborne Wharf 2000. Old FMC Warehouse conversion

It is a regrettable fact that most canalside heritage structures have disappeared from the BCN waterfront. Those that remain have found other uses. The Fellows, Morton & Clayton warehouse at Sherborne Street Wharf was constructed during 1938 to replace their establishment at the Crescent. The building passed to British Waterways, but ceased to have any canal role once carrying had ceased on the waterway. The building remained unaltered until the mid-1990s but has subsequently been converted into residential apartments. Substantial structural alterations were made to the building during the conversion.

Sheepcote Street Bridge, Oozells Loop, 2000

The making of a new pathway along the Oozells Street branch also followed the conversion of Sherborne Street Warehouse to Sherborne Street Wharf. This work was conducted as part of continuing improvements that have revitalised the canal here.

Reliving the past at Birchills Top Lock
Canal restoration and preservation takes many forms. In this view Trevor Hale and Ann Stevens are seen wearing traditional boat dress at a Birchills boat gathering. The boat is the Fellows, Morton & Clayton MV, the *Minnow*.

The steamboat President *at the IWA Rally, Netherton, 1996*
Canal boat restoration requires a considerable dedication to achieve the correct result. *President* has received its share of attention since it was purchased from British Waterways. The steamboat *President* was constructed at the FMC Saltley Boat Dock in 1909 where it was fitted with a Haines steam engine and a Ruston Proctor boiler. *President* joined the FMC fleet that operated principally along the Grand Union Canal between Birmingham or Leicester and London. FMC took the steam engine power unit out in 1925 and fitted a conventional Bolinder engine. It stayed a motorboat for the rest of its working life ending it with British Waterways North West fleet. The boat was restored to its original steamboat state, although the power unit was not of the Haines design. It is probable that none have survived.

Steamboats President, *the* Kildare*, and canoes at Malthouse Stables, Tipton*
President and the butty *Kildare* are seen at Tipton on an outing from the Black Country Museum, where they are now based. *Kildare* was built at the West Bromwich boatyard of Braithwaite & Kirk in 1913 and has been restored to pristine original condition by the trust that now owns the *President*.

Dudley Canal Trust Electric Tunnel Boat at Tipton, 1998
The Dudley Canal Trust deserves credit for the restoration of the Dudley Tunnel. They run regular trips through the limestone caverns from the Black Country Museum Wharf using a fleet of specially built craft. They also operate trips along the tunnel to Blowers Green Pump House, which is now the headquarters of the trust. One boat is seen at Tipton after bringing members of the Railway & Canal Historical Society through the tunnel from Parkhead.

Coronation Gardens, Tipton
The coronation of Queen Elizabeth II gave rise to the naming of these canalside gardens at Tipton. Old wharves were levelled to make the new amenity.

Round's Timber Yard
One of the few surviving examples of canalside industry is W. Round's timber yard at Tipton. Here seasoning timber can still be seen stacked beside the waterway. It is a reminder of a time when timber was carried by boat to timber yards.

Commercial Wharf, Horseleyfields
The archway under the railway viaduct still leads to wharf stable block that served Crowley &
Co. and later the Shropshire Union Railway & Canal Carrying Co.

Regeneration Oozells Loop.
The regeneration of canalside property in Birmingham has been now in progress for a decade.
Former industrial premises in Sheepcote Street are seen in the process of demolition and the
canal under reconstruction to provide make new residential properties and improved moorings
for boats.

Titford Pools 2002, clearing canal
Canalside maintenance requires constant attention. British Waterways find help in this area from organisations such as the Birmingham Canal Navigations Society, whose members help at clean up events. On Saturday 9 February 2002, students from Great Barr School are seen assisting the Birmingham Canal Navigations Society workboat *Phoenix*, clearing rubbish from Titford Pools.

Fishing at the Canal Anglesey Arm
Canals now provide opportunity for many leisure pursuits. Walking, cycling and fishing are now regular activities in which people can participate.

Fountain Inn, Tipton
Canalside inns are part of canal heritage. The Fountain in Owen Street once had stables for the boat horses and provided food and drink for the boatmen.

Gospel Oak branch, 1979.
The Gospel Oak branch joined the Walsall Canal at Leabrook. For many years the principal traffic was associated with Willingsworth Furnaces that lay close to its route. Willingsworth Furnaces ceased to be used in the 1920s but were not demolished until 1942. This photograph shows the site after clearance. The remains of the former slag bank are still visible, as is the ribbon of water that comprised the disused branch. Since this picture was taken, most the branch has been filled in and converted to a public walkway.

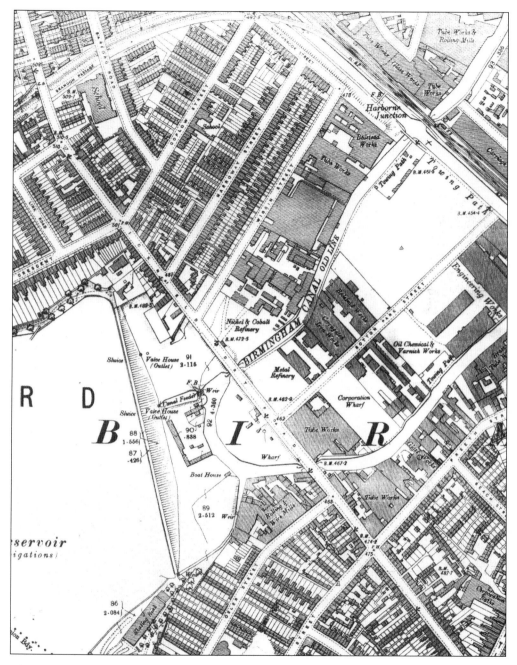

Icknield Port Loop. Reproduced from Second Ordnance Survey, surveyed 1902.
The Icknield Port Loop comprised part of the route of the Old Birmingham Canal. It followed the land contours following one side of a valley before crossing over to the other. The construction of the New Main Line created an area of valley land totally enclosed by canal. Gradually this land was made up to canal level that was hastened by the making of a new thoroughfare, Icknield Port Road. As the land was reclaimed, it was taken over by new industrial development that included an engineering works (Bellis & Morcam), a varnish works (Docker Brothers) and a metal refinery (McKecknie Brothers).

Icknield Port Loop as seen from Edgbaston Reservoir

The Icknield Port Loop received water from Edgbaston Reservoir whose dam towers high above the waterway. In this 1995 photograph the view from the top of the dam looks down on the canal maintenance yard across old stable blocks to the canal and a range of buildings that line the canal on the opposite side. The making of Icknield Port Road had led to the establishment of a canal company wharf on the land between the road and the inside of the loop. This wharf, which can be seen on the reproduced part of the 1902 ordnance survey map, was used by a number of coal merchants. Part was later given over to factory development, but these premises were levelled during the 1990s restoring the open space that had been the original Icknield Port Wharf.